Hitting The Mark

The A-B-C's Of Rating Customers & Sales Leads

Hitting The Mark

The A-B-C's Of Rating Customers & Sales Leads

Steve Hoffacker

CAPS, MCSP, MIRM

Hitting The Mark

The A-B-C's Of Rating Customers & Sales Leads

Cover photo by Steve Hoffacker.

ALL RIGHTS RESERVED.

© 2014, 2010 by Hoffacker Associates LLC
West Palm Beach, Florida, USA
ISBN: 978-0-9843524-4-9

Each customer or sales lead that you approach or that comes to you has different needs and requirements. Some are able to make decisions quickly while others need weeks — or even months or years — to make a decision. Some will never make a decision. Devoting the same amount of time or energy to working with each customer or sales lead is not a wise, productive, or efficient use of your resources. Knowing who to focus on and work with is the key.

Other Aging-In-Place & Universal Design Sales Books By Steve Hoffacker

Find additional books (softbound print editions and Kindle eBooks) by Steve Hoffacker on aging-in-place, universal design, or remodeling/contractor sales at http:stevehoffacker.com/aginginplacesalesbooks.html):

"**Power Of Discovery:** *Who, What, When, Where, & More In Building The Sale*"

"**Mining Your Database:** *Making More Sales Through People You Already Know*"

"**Filling Your Funnel:** *Building Your Business By Reaching Out To Strangers*"

"**Universal Design For Builders:** *Building & Selling Accessible, Safe & Comfortable New Homes*"

"**Common Sense Universal Design:** *Creating Accessible, Safe, Comfortable & Desirable Homes*"

"**Universal Design And Aging:** *Keeping Our Homes Safe, Accessible & Comfortable As We Age In Place*"

"**Universal Design For Safety:** *Creating Safe & Accessible Living Spaces For All Ages*"

Table Of Contents

Chapter	Page

Preface 13

1. Why You Need A Rating System 19

    Everyone Has Their Own Agenda 19
    People Have Different Needs 20
    Don't Rely On Repeated Contacts 21
    Why You Need A Rating System 22
    Go With The Written System 24
    The Reason For Assigning A Mark 25
    What The Mark Really Means 26
    The Mark Is Not Personal 27
    Determining Who Needs Your Time 27
    Relying On A Rating System 29
    Selecting A Good Rating System 30
    An Essential Sales Tool 31

2. The "Ready, Willing, And Able" Test 33

    The "A-B-C" Rating System 33
    The Importance Of An Objective Test 34

Creating The Objective Test 35
The "Ready, Willing, And Able" Test 36
The "Ready" Factor 37
The "Readiness" Question 39
The "Influencer" Factor 41
The "Willing" Component 43
The Status Quo Dilemma 45
The Importance Of "Willingness" 46
Elimination Of "Buyer's Remorse" 48
The "Willingness" Question 50
The "Able" Variable 52
The "Able" Test 53
There Must be Full Payment 54
Looks Can Be Deceiving 55
Remaining Objective 56
Getting Consistent Results 57
Putting It All Together 59

3. An "A" Rating Isn't Sufficient 61

Committing To A Rating System 61
Identifying Your Top Possibilities 62
Using the "A-B-C" Rating System 63
Adding A "D" To The Rating System 65
Adjusting Your Rating System 66
Effort Is Not The Answer 67
Introducing The "A-1" Rating 68
Refining The Traditional Rating System 69
Applying The "A-1" Rating Objectively 70
Giving You An Edge With Your Time 71

Table Of Contents

    Hoarding Isn't The Answer 72
    People Are Subject To Change 73
    An "A-1" *Is* Special 73
    The True "A-1" Customer 75
    Enjoying Success With The "A-1" 75
    Special Contact For Your "A"s 76
    Adding Your Congratulations 77
    Focusing On Your "A"s Again 78
    Rating With All Four Factors 79

4. Going Behind The Mark 81

    Knowing The Rating Possibilities 81
    Applying The "A" Mark 82
    Applying The "A-1" Mark 83
    Applying The "B" Mark 85
    Applying The "B-1" Mark 86
    Applying The "C" Mark 87
    Applying The "C-1" Mark 89
    Applying The "D" Mark 90
    Applying The "D-1" Mark 91
    At-A-Glance Marking Summary 92

5. Only A Few Can Be An "A-1" 95

    The Importance Of Your "A-1"s 95
    You Need To Be Intentional 96
    Contact Other Than Face-To-Face 97
    Working Efficiently 99
    Initial Post-Visit Contact 100

Verifying Your Initial Rating 102
An Exception To The Rule 103
Amending The Rating 104
Scheduling Your Time 105
Maintaining Your Focus 106
You'll Only Close An "A-1" 107
You Can't Force It 108
People's Situations Can Change 109

6. Don't Discount The "D"s 111

What A "D" Rating Means 111
A "D" Customer Is Not "Able" 112
Reasons For A "D" Rating 112
Keeping It In Perspective 114
A "D" Rating Can Change 115
When The "D" Rating Changes 116
"D" Actually Means "D-1" 117
Looking At The Bigger Picture 119
Being Strategic With Your "D-1"s 120
Maintaining Appropriate Contact 121
The Purpose Of Your Contact 122

7. Marking Outside The Lines 123

Other Types Of Contacts 123
Recording The Contacts 124
The Trades 125
Professionals 126
Brokers 127

Table Of Contents

Third-Party 128
Other 129
Telephone Contacts 130
Obtaining Value From The Calls 130
Email Inquiries 131

8. **Getting The Most From Your Customers & Sales Leads** **133**

Using Your Rating System 133
Stop Chasing After People 135
Maximizing Your Effort 136
Be Honest With Your Ratings 138
The Race Against The Clock 139
The 30-Day Buying Cycle 141
Planning For Your "A-1"s 142
Managing The Rest Of Your Database 143
The Real Pay-Off 145

Preface

I appreciate that you bought this book and that you are reading and using it.

It shows that you are interested in being an even better remodeler, trade contractor, occupational therapist, DME supplier, architect, or other aging-in-place or universal design provider — whether you are doing the estimating, sales, or assessments personally or you are overseeing them.

This book is going to revolutionize the way you work with your customers, how you approach and make sales, and how you schedule your activities.

It's going to energize you and give you a fresh perspective on managing and allocating your time and deciding how to work with your customer base.

You'll be able to be much more strategic in how you conduct your initial presentations, subsequent contacts, and return appointments.

We know that the sales process begins when someone contacts you by phone or email or when they visit your office or showroom — or you approach them.

Not all clients, customers, and sales leads are created the same, however.

They differ in terms of their interest level, needs, requirements, capacity to like or want what you're offering or what you have to show them, and their ability to make a decision — as well as how quickly any decision is likely to happen.

Some customers will be "just getting ideas" when you meet with them or they visit you.

Others will need to make a decision immediately.

Some will want to put it out to bid. Others just want to careful and will take their time in reaching a decision — if one is forthcoming at all

A few will show no interest at all in what you have, and you'll wonder why they even visited or contacted you.

How then do you decide which people are the most serious while you're working or talking with them?

Who should be re-contacted right away, and who may not need any immediate consideration?

Who needs additional attention after you leave them or they depart your showroom or office — and which ones require very little or no more contact?

Preface

In this book, I offer specific ways for you to determine which customers or sales leads are the most deserving of your time and attention and which are likely not to purchase anything from you — no matter what you do.

The latter will not require much, if any, of your time after you initially meet or talk with them.

This way you'll know which ones to focus on and how to manage your time and resources quite well.

The basis for this efficiency is an effective rating system that determines and ascertains each customer's, client's, and sales lead's ability and willingness to make a decision and prioritizes them accordingly.

This system focuses on using the decision date as the key indicator.

The delivery, installation, commencement, or anticipated completion date is less important.

Obviously, those who are able to make a decision the quickest are your best opportunities for a sale or engagement and the ones you'll want to concentrate on first, but there is a little more to it than just focusing on these people.

In this book, I will reveal and explain the best, most effective grading system for all of your contacts and leads.

No other rating system is necessary.

Every single person, company, or customer unit who contacts or visits you — or the ones you contact — regardless of their level of interest in acquiring or using your services can be accommodated by this system.

As a result of reading this book and implementing my system, you will be a much more efficient and productive salesperson, sales manager, professional, contractor, or business owner.

You'll be able to prioritize your customers and sales leads and determine appropriate courses of action, based on their ability to make a decision.

This book is for remodelers and general contractors, trade contractors, occupational and physical therapists, architects, DME companies, building materials supply and manufacturing companies, interior designers, kitchen and bath designers, non-profit agencies and associations, and anyone involved in supplying or meeting the needs of people with aging-in-place requirements or general functional renovation with attention to safety and comfort.

Hitting The Mark

The A-B-C's Of Rating Customers & Sales Leads

1

Why You Need A Rating System

Everyone Has Their Own Agenda

People come in all sizes, abilities, and needs. They have different life experiences and backgrounds. They shop for products and services in various ways, with no two sales presentations being identical. They have different desires for their homes, renovation requirements and ideas, agendas, timing, and budgets.

Some of the people who contact you by phone, email, or a visit to your showroom, office, or trade show/home show booth — or those you meet or contact on your own — will have more immediate needs than others, regardless of any type of specific interest they express or convey in what you are providing.

Some will have almost no interest in acting at all.

Just from initial impressions, it may not be that easy to tell which of your potential customers or sales leads are interested in working with you and those that are not.

More than one meeting or conversation may be necessary before you determine how serious someone is, and then several meetings may be required before the scope of work is actually settled.

People Have Different Needs

Because people have different needs, interest levels, and timing for making their decisions — as well as budgets — giving everyone the same presentation about you, your company, your services or products, the benefits of what you offer and the way you approach your work, specific solutions that you might recommend, or quality or life expectancy of their investment will have vastly different results.

For those people that actually are looking for a solution and are serious about making a decision, the sooner you discover their motivations and learn what their real agenda is, the quicker you can begin helping them find a solution that will meet their needs — and their budget.

Still, depending on the urgency and the medical necessity of what they need, their decision as to what to do and how to proceed could be mean that any potential purchase or agreement with you could be months away.

Therefore, devoting the same amount of time to working with everyone — and especially committing a lot of time to working with those who never are going to be making a decision — is not a productive, effective, or efficient use of your time.

Don't Rely On Repeated Contacts

Sometimes it's those people who have no intention or desire of ever making a decision who keep calling you, emailing you, or dropping in to ask you to show them your products or discuss your services again.

They may ask for new pricing data, change their desired scope or specifications, ask for another bid, request duplicate information for someone else to review, or reiterate their apparent interest in doing something.

Just because someone keeps showing apparent interest by continuing to contact you or asking questions by telephone or email doesn't necessarily mean that they will eventually buy anything from you.

In fact, the opposite is probably true.

You'd like to think that when people contact or reach out to you again and again that it means that they really like you, what you offer, and the products, services, or solutions that you offer and that you have discussed with them. That isn't always the case.

Some people will have a good understanding of what they want and how you desire to approach their needs during their first telephone conversation with you or on your initial presentation, but many will take more than one contact before they acquire this comfort level.

So just having someone who returns to your office to meet with you, calls you on the phone, texts or emails you, and asks you to show them more solutions, modify your proposal, check on pricing information, or conduct additional research on their questions are not necessarily buying signs in themselves. It may even indicate that a sale or order is not likely or possible.

You may have noticed that some people will contact you frequently, continue to visit your office or showroom, allow you to call upon them, respond to your emails, or otherwise appear to stay involved with you yet never seem ready to make a decision — while even others who seem to show a lot of interest in what you offer will end up buying from a competitor.

Why You Need A Rating System

Because people visiting or contacting you — or allowing you to maintain contact with them — have their own agendas, needs, desires, requirements, budgets, timetables, criteria, levels of interest, and capacities or abilities to make a decision, you need a way of keeping tabs on the most interested ones at any given time.

I know that some salespeople can remember and retain information about all of their customers or at least the good sales leads in their heads — maybe you're one of them.

They can recall every important detail about their customers and manage all of the communication details that are necessary to produce a sale or order.

However, even at this, it's challenging to prioritize which customers require more attention than others without continually mentally reviewing each individual customer — one at a time. This can be time consuming.

It gets trickier over time as you meet more people and field telephone inquiries and email requests from potential customers and sales leads.

As we get older and as we continue to see and talk with more and more people, our ability to keep track of everyone and all of the little details about each customer or sales lead in our heads becomes more of an issue.

Thus, one option is to continue to use a mental rating system where you attempt to remember who you're working, what needs to be done with each one — especially those you consider to be the best — and where they are in their decision-making process. That is, if you ever had this ability at all.

Or, you can create a written system that eliminates the chance that someone may slip through the cracks.

The degree of formality and amount of detail in your system is entirely up to up — and possibly your company — but I believe you should have a basic rating system.

Personally and professionally, I recommend the *written* system over a less formal approach.

Go With The Written System

Your system doesn't need to be *computerized,* and it doesn't need to be expensive to create or implement. However, you do need some formal way of writing down and keeping track of the contact information and other details about leads and people you've met.

Regardless of how many people you might be working with at any given time, the best way to make sure that you haven't forgotten any important details or anything that needs to be done or scheduled is to write it down.

Then, you need to have a way of assigning a grade, mark, score, or some type of rating to each customer.

This is how you'll indicate which ones are the closest to making a purchasing decision, which ones are more distant, and which ones probably will never make a decision — regardless of how interested they may seem.

Without a written record of each lead or customer, you'll find that making notes, assigning ratings, and keeping track of their progress is nearly impossible.

The Reason For Assigning A Mark

You need to assign a grade, mark, rating, or rank to all of your customers and sales leads to help you prioritize and identify where each person is in their decision-making process, but there's nothing special or magical about the actual score or mark that you use or assign.

It's what the rating or mark indicates.

The reason that that you grade, mark, or rank each customer is to allow you to immediately identify and then focus on those customers who are the most likely at any given time to be in a position to make a decision to purchase your services.

Think of the mark as a type of shorthand or notation that will tell you at a glance just how likely someone is to purchase from you — and more specifically where that next sale might be coming from.

It also allows other people in your company — an associate, assistant, manager, supervisor, or office staff — to use your notes and assist you in talking with a particular customer on your behalf when you're busy with other customers or away from the office.

Be diligent in deciding on which mark to assign to each customer.

The better the mark, the more likely, and quicker, the decision — but only if it truly is representative of their interest level and ability to make a decision.

You should never force or exaggerate a mark just for the sake of appearances.

It's just that simple.

What The Mark Really Means

There are many systems in use around the country for keeping track of how *"good"* someone is.

You may already have an informal system — such as "A-B-C," "1-2-3," "hot-warm-cold," or something similar — to differentiate your customers and indicate the apparent quality of your traffic and leads.

It may be your own system — something you created — where you just color-code or put a checkmark on the "good" ones. Maybe you just remember the good ones.

Regardless of which system you use, however, the best score, rating, or mark would indicate which customers are the closest to making a purchasing decision at any given moment.

The grade or mark only reflects someone's willingness or ability to make a decision — and nothing else.

However, understanding their willingness and ability to purchase what you offer, and have you get started fulfilling their request, is huge.

The Mark Is Not Personal

The rating must not be based on anything personal.

It has nothing to do with your customers personally. It has nothing to do with how well you might like or relate to someone — or much they might "need" what you provide.

It refers *solely* to the general likelihood of them making a decision — and the approximate timing of it.

It shouldn't focus on their personality, how they dress, the car they drive, what you might have in common with them, how well you interact with them, what company they are part of, their attitude, the quality of their home, or how nice you think they are as a person.

Determining Who Needs Your Time

When you meet or talk with a new customer or potential sales lead for the first time, you ask them questions and discuss their needs, requirements, timing, budget, expectations, and desired outcome.

This might be in your office, their home (sitting in their living room or at the kitchen or dining room table), on the telephone when they call for information, or by email when someone contacts you through your website.

It could be from a trade or home show, a referral, or some other type of advertising or promotion.

Beginning with that initial contact, you need a way of noting or remembering which customers or leads are sincerely interested in doing something — and more specifically working with you.

Which people should you devote more time to and actively pursue because they are likely to purchase or acquire something from you?

Conversely, which customers or sales leads need minimal or virtually no contact because they have no interest in doing anything — or a decision seems unlikely?

How can you differentiate the levels of interest among your customers or sales leads after your initial conversation or discussion with them?

The answers to these questions are found in effectively rating each customer according to their willingness and ability to make a purchasing decision in favor of what you are offering — and more specifically doing it with you and your company.

Relying On A Rating System

As a contractor, estimator, occupational therapist doing assessments, or anyone else working in someone's home, you need a simple, effective rating system that allows you to determine very quickly who to focus on and continue working with after the initial meeting.

Then you can commit and plan your time to work with just those customers or leads who have the highest probability of making a decision on what you offer.

While your memory may be great, you really do need a way of reviewing and managing your customer base — something you can look at frequently.

This is why you need to have a formal, written system of keeping track of your customers and sales leads — even if it's just in a 3-ring notebook or on notecards in a cardboard file box.

In addition, there are many CRM software programs available to help you keep track of your customers.

However, they're no *substitute* for knowing how to supply the appropriate grade or mark to each customer based upon your interaction with each one and the answers they provide to your discovery questions about their needs, preferences, level of interest, timing, budget, expectations, and ability to act.

Remember that it's the person doing the rating — you — and how the ratings are used that's important, and not whether the actual customer records are stored in a file drawer, notebook, or on a computer.

Selecting A Good Rating System

Make sure you select a good rating system, and the one that I'll show you in the coming pages is the best for several reasons that you'll see as I explain it.

A good rating system will allow you to identify and work with those people closest to making a decision at any given time — as well as those who need a little "hand-holding" along the way.

You'll also be able to identify those people who essentially require no additional contact from you.

Many people will have no interest in purchasing anything in the near term or ever — and you may even wonder why they contacted or met with you, unless they were just doing casual research or just dreaming.

Others will require minimal contact over several months or even longer before a decision is ever likely.

Why would you want to invest much of your time in working with or pursuing these people when you know that your efforts would be more productive elsewhere?

Your rating system will let you prioritize your follow-up activity, and you can devote more time to working with those people who need your help and encouragement to make a decision.

By using your rating system to identify where remodeling, renovation, or other aging-in-place decisions are the most likely to happen, you will be able to make sales that otherwise might be overlooked or go unmade because you lost track of them — thereby avoiding a loss to you, your company, and the customer or client.

An Essential Sales Tool

The rating system is not something that is just nice to have.

It is an essential sales and management tool.

A rating system allows you to keep track of where everyone is in their search for what you offer — from very close to making a decision to likely never to make a decision.

It lets you prioritize your time and your efforts to focus on working with those customers closest to making a decision.

When you have written information on your customers, clients, or sales leads, you can your review your individual customer ratings and notes as often as you like and update them as necessary — changing the grade or mark up or down as appropriate.

This takes all of the guesswork out of identifying the people most likely to purchase with you — and lets you determine those that you can effectively set aside.

It truly allows you to focus on working with people who have the highest probability of making a decision with you — whether that decision is imminent or weeks, months, or even years away.

2

The "Ready, Willing, And Able" Test

The "A-B-C" Rating System

A common form of a customer rating and tracking system in use in many sales businesses across the country is the one known as the "A-B-C" system.

In this format, the "A" designates the top quality or those most-likely-to-make a decision, and "C" the least ready — with "B" somewhere in between. Sometimes, there is a "D" or other letters used also.

However, there are wide variations as to what constitutes each grade and how they are applied. For instance, what may be an "A" to one salesperson or company may not be to another.

Often there are differences — and sometimes disagreements — within the same company, department, agency, or organization as to what each letter grade means and why someone should receive a certain grade and not another.

This variance and uncertainty underscores the need for an objective rating system rather than a subjective one.

The Importance Of An Objective Test

The ratings and the rating system should not be based on anything personal and must not be reflective of someone's personality or demeanor.

A rating system must remain objective.

If anyone else in your company or your office, such as your manager or assistant, were to review your notes on any particular customer or sales lead, they should arrive at essentially the same mark or rating as you have for that person.

It may not be that way today, but that's the aim of an objective rating or scoring system.

There just is no room for subjectivity.

This will undermine a rating system quicker than anything else — except not using one at all.

The ratings must be consistently applied to your entire customer database and be based solely on an objective set of measurable criteria that reflect someone's ability to make a decision and how soon that might happen.

Your emotions or personal views can't have anything to do with the ratings.

We're all human, and some of our feelings may creep into how we interpret someone's ability and willingness, but to the extent possible, we need to be objective in our approach.

Creating The Objective Test

If the ratings that we use to evaluate the interest level and decision-making ability of our customers, clients, and sales leads are truly objective, they should be true regardless of who the customers are and who is doing the rating. If you rate your database, or I do it, we should come up with roughly the same ratings.

One of the best tests to use to objectively determine the status of your customers and sales leads is known as the *"ready, willing, and able"* test.

While the "A-B-C" system is so often used to reflect this ready, willing and able assessment or test, there often is general confusion about what constitutes these three attributes and how to apply them.

This is largely true because they aren't viewed as the objective measurement that they really are.

The "Ready, Willing, And Able" Test

The foundation of any good rating system is an objective set of criteria.

The best set of criteria I've found for determining someone's likelihood of making a purchasing decision or deciding to use your services is the *"ready, willing, and able"* test.

It turns out that each of the three measures ("ready," "willing," and "able") indicates someone's *preparedness* or *capacity* to make a decision, and each of these can be quantified.

That is, each can be measured *objectively* as to whether it has been met — without any subjectivity being necessary.

This is the real power of this system.

So, instead of just having a "good" or "not-so-good" feeling about someone and their ability to make a purchasing decision with you, you actually can assess their ability on an objective basis.

And, if it's truly an objective assessment, then any

salesperson, estimator, contractor, manager, or assistant who evaluates the "ready, willing, and able" criteria of a particular customer should arrive at essentially the same conclusion concerning their ability to make a decision and the timing of that decision.

The "Ready" Factor

The first test in the measurement trilogy is "READY," and this is a *physical* issue.

This means that in order for someone to be considered "ready" to make a decision on your product, service, design, or proposal they need to be *physically* prepared to do so — and to have it delivered, installed, or commenced without delay.

Their current home or office (in the case of commercial renovations or ADA improvements) or its present condition will not be an excuse or determining factor in making their decision.

Waiting on completion of a do-it-yourself fix-up, repair, or painting currently underway or contemplated by them will not be a reason to delay their decision.

It simply won't inhibit a decision.

In the case of a medical device, air filtration, heating or air conditioning, other mechanical systems, or major appliances for which they might have a warranty or service policy arrangement that they are not relying on continuing to use a product that falls under such a warranty or service plan as being an excuse or limiting factor in deciding to go ahead and acquire or commence what you offer or suggest.

They can continue to use what they have in addition to what you are selling them, they can cancel or terminate their current arrangement, or they can make a decision now to go with you because the term of their current service is almost at an end.

Depending on what appliances, products, or services you are selling, the delivery date might be such that a purchasing decision can be made now for a later delivery or installation of your product — or the effective date is weeks or months away.

This means that there is plenty of time to phase out what they have now prior to taking delivery or commencing with your product or service.

It also means that deciding to make improvements commercially to their office or plant will not inhibit or delay making a decision on your new product or service.

It also means that nothing needs to happen first. There are no physical constraints to moving forward — such as completion and approval of an application, an existing lease, getting the space prepared or cleaned out, or meeting regulations or rules governing how a property can be used, improved, or developed.

This is how the "ready" test is applied and what it means.

It really is that simple.

The "Readiness" Question

To test someone's "readiness" to make a decision, you need to determine if they can actually proceed with entering into an agreement with you or saying "yes" to your proposed solution without relying, deferring, or depending on anything else factoring into that decision.

This means that their present home or leased space (in the case of an office or commercial or industrial space), physical condition of their home or facility, and any products or services with a useful lifespan that they currently are using would not be a reason or consideration for not going ahead with their decision.

Notice that the key to whether this test is accomplished is the ability of someone to make the decision.

The test does not depend on the timing or ability of people to close on the sale, take delivery, have the equipment or technology installed, or commence the services you're offering. It's just whether the decision can be made.

You're only looking for someone who can give you an initial deposit, full deposit, design/build agreement, purchase order, handshake, or signed scope of services agreement without falling back on their present situation as factoring into or governing that decision.

This is all that you need to satisfy the "ready" criteria — regardless of how your product, service, or solution is to be delivered or conveyed to them.

People are still free complete improvements to their facility that aren't part of what you offer, or to phase out or continue using products or services that yours will replace, complement, or supplement. The key is that making a decision with you is not dependent on those actions occurring first.

When you ask someone you're working with to purchase your product or service or the design solutions you are presenting, you don't want to hear them tell you: "*I need to use up what I have on hand first,*" or "*I have to wait until our current inventory is exhausted before I can do anything,*" or "*I still have several months to go on my current plan,*" or "*After we complete our current lease, we'll be in a position to look at what you have,*" or "*We'll have to see if we can get out of (terminate) our lease (service or product) first.*"

As long as you don't hear anything about a current situation that prevents or delays them from considering and moving forward with the purchase or acquisition of what you offer, they are "ready" to make a decision.

The "Influencer" Factor

Another part of the readiness determination is the capacity or ability of the person you are talking with about the decision to actually be able to make it.

In the case of a business, you might be meeting with the operations manager, plant supervisor, vice president of operations, sales manager, marketing director, purchasing director, HR director, CEO, CFO, COO, president, accountant, comptroller, facilities manager, risk management, corporate attorney, or the actual small business owner.

In the case of consumers, you likely are meeting with the household head, whether a renter or owner, or their partner or spouse — or both. It could be an adult child or children, someone with power of attorney for such decisions, or an administrator of a trust.

Working with an influencer or someone other than the client is quite likely in the case of someone with cognitive issues or a traumatic injury that leaves them incapable of participating in the discussion and planning for the renovation.

Working with a business to provide services for them could involve several people from outside the company also.

This would include attorneys, accountants, financial planners and advisors, engineers, architects, other contractors, consultants, insurance agents, and other professionals — as well as spouses, knowledgeable friends, former employees, or citizen or consumer task forces or advisory group members — who might offer their advice about the need for, budget, and anticipated outcome for remodeling, renovation, expansion, or replacement of existing products or fixtures.

If the person you are talking with can't make the decision without deferring to others in the organization or the family, or having it reviewed by various departments or committees, he or she is deemed not ready to make a decision.

If you hear anything like the following — from a business or a consumer — they are not "ready" to make a decision: *"The facilities committee will have to review this first,"* or *"We need to send this out for(get at least 3) bids before we can do anything,"* *"We'll have to let (have) our board of directors (architect, consultant, engineer, accountant) look at this before we can commit to anything,"* or *"We'll have to see if we can get the zoning we want first,"* or *"You'll have to get on our vendors list before we can have a serious discussion* about moving ahead," or "We'll have to let our accountants go over and review any numbers that you give us before we can commit to anything," or "We'll have to check with our cousin (aunt, uncle, brother, sister, parents, best friend, in-laws, neighbor, co-worker, attorney, accountant) first before we can do anything like this."

They are conveniently deferring to others to delay or forestall a decision — clearly an indication that they are not ready to proceed.

The "Willing" Component

The second part of the three-step rating formula is "WILLING." This is an *emotional* or *psychological* factor or measurement.

Someone needs to be emotionally or psychologically prepared to make the decision on getting something new or redoing what they have because they *definitely* have decided to make a change. They "need" it and are prepared to make the decision to say "yes."

In the case of a traumatic change, it's still something that's necessary and that can't be put off while it is put out for bids.

Otherwise, they have decided that what they have now just isn't working and they no longer wish to continue this way.

Maybe they have come to this decision recently, and possibly it has been a long time in coming. Nevertheless, what they are using now or they current floor plan layout no longer addresses their present situation effectively.

Maybe what they have now is outdated or obsolete. It might even be dangerous.

It's no longer just a case of *"thinking about"* or wishing for a solution or something new but actually *needing* it. They have moved from the *"nice to have"* to the *"must have."*

It's no longer a case of just talking about doing something or just shopping around to see what's available. It's now a must-do situation — at least emotionally if not physically.

They have passed the point of doing casual research, collecting brochures, or talking with people such as you about what could be. They are actively doing research on a solution for their current needs.

When someone makes the emotional commitment to move on from where they are or what they have now, the purchase will happen — and usually rather quickly.

This is true whether it's a retooling of existing space or

new construction of an addition or expansion space — for residential or commercial purposes.

The Status Quo Dilemma

When someone is "willing" to purchase new appliances, cabinets, flooring, lighting, or fixtures to replace, complement, supplement, or update what they have now — or reconfigure, redo, modernize, or expand their current layout or design — they will have passed the point-of-no-return, and keeping things as they are will not be a viable option.

It won't even be a consideration.

Up until the point when the "willingness" factor has been satisfied, many people will gauge what they see available online and in the marketplace against what they are currently using or doing.

They'll be evaluating, comparing, and interpreting what they see or experience in light of their present situation and what it will take to replace it, redo it, or modernize it from a financial, environmental, life-cycle, comfort, sustainability, value, features, benefits, efficiency, size, complexity, and convenience standpoint or basis.

Until the willingness factor has been satisfied, their current layout and functional systems often will look more attractive or appealing to them than anything else they've considered or that you might show them.

Sometimes, it's just a matter of not wanting to make any changes or leaving well enough alone — even though what they have is inadequate or unsatisfactory.

It might also be a case of knowing what they have now, along with all its warts and shortcomings, versus a learning curve and unknown territory in making changes.

As a result, they may decide just to stay the course with what they have and to give up the idea of making any changes — even if they would benefit from the changes and really might desire and enjoy them.

The Importance Of "Willingness"

"Willingness" is the most crucial test of someone's ability to make a decision.

Of course, being "ready" and "able" are important parts of assessing how likely, prepared, or capable someone is to make a purchasing decision.

It's just that the decision won't happen — or it won't survive second thoughts, cancellation, or rescission — unless someone is emotionally willing to make it.

This makes "willing" the *pivotal test* in measuring how likely a sale is to occur.

It's what you need to look for the most. It's what you need for a decision to happen.

You must identify it to have a successful transaction.

You must have all — and not just some — of the decision-makers or influential parties on-board with the need for action before a successful decision can be made. Any "foot-draggers" could delay a decision.

As I discussed in making the "ready" determination, if the key decision-maker you are talking to is not prepared to make a binding decision for the company or the family, you won't get one.

There could be accountants, financial planners, investment brokers, boards of directors, spouses, partners, purchasing agents, consultants, attorneys, insurance agents, friends, relatives, or others who will factor into the decision — directly or indirectly through their influence or advice.

Thus, everyone involved in signing-off on the decision to improve the property (residential or commercial) must be onboard with the decision — there has to be a collective meeting of the minds on the part of your customer before you can obtain a purchasing decision.

In the emotional impact of the moment as you are helping your customers get excited about the possibilities of making the changes you are describing and laying out for them, they may join in your excitement and decide to move forward.

However, if they weren't already "willing" or predisposed to make that decision before they met with you and made it simply on impulse or because of their temporary excitement in how you were presenting your plan, they most likely will cancel or rescind their decision within a day or two.

Elimination Of "Buyer's Remorse"

The concept of *"buyer's remorse"* — where people decide to cancel or rescind their decision after you leave them and they're alone to rethink or second-guess what they have done — should never be a serious issue for you if the people you are selling to are emotionally prepared to make their decisions and have made it intentionally without any undue pressure being applied or inferred.

If they truly are "willing" to make that purchasing decision when you are working with them, then it won't be a case of them feeling pressured or talked into doing something that they weren't prepared to do.

While people might decide that a different company or supplier could meet their needs as well as or better than what they have selected with you, that they really couldn't afford their purchase or can't justify it fiscally ("able"), or that they really should have shopped for a better price or terms more to their liking, they generally won't cancel a purchase for remorse if they were emotionally ready ("willing") to make the decision in the first place.

Occasionally, you'll run into a situation where — after you've done all the work and prepared them for the close, possibly even getting a signed order or purchase agreement — they'll cancel because they find out that someone who is somehow related to or best friends with a decision-maker comes to the party late and wants to the work for them — possibly at a better price due to the relationship.

There is little you can do to anticipate this or overcome it. Still, they were willing to make the decision, which is the key.

Until people are emotionally, psychologically, or intently prepared ("willing") to purchase something for a need they have, the other two criteria — "ready" and "able" — are not that important.

The decision to purchase may be based on any number of factors and considerations, but there must be a psychological or emotional basis for that decision.

Some people may act or process information more from a logical or analytical perspective, but a purchasing decision is largely an emotional decision.

That's why the "willingness" part of the equation is the central measure.

To have a truly happy and excited client or customer, they have to be emotionally and psychologically prepared to say "*yes*" to what you're offering them. This will largely eliminate any feelings of regret about the decision.

The "ready" and "able" factors are important, but "willing" is the key to the decision.

The "Willingness" Question

No matter how much someone "thinks" that they want to get a new addition, have their space remodeled or updated, or accommodate the needs of any of the household members such as you offer — or how many times they revisit the various websites to look at them again or even contact you again to discuss what you offer — and how prepared or able they might seem to make a decision, the real issue is how much they "want" or "need" to have what you offer. Of course, the need is stronger with mobility issues or other medical concerns.

When someone sees something that they like that meets their needs — regardless of whether they initiated the contact with you or you called on them, and whether they expected to like you and your solution well enough to get started — can they say "*yes*"?

The "Ready, Willing, And Able" Test

This is the real issue; this is how the "willing" test is applied.

To be "willing" to make a decision they need to have made the mental or emotional commitment to acquire or purchase what you offer — or at least to do something to solve their issues — *before* meeting or talking with you.

If someone hasn't definitely decided to buy whatever you're offering before you meet with them — whether they eventually purchase from you or a competitor — there will no purchasing decision at that time.

Many people will contact you or allow you to meet with them, and you'll wonder why they even made the effort or agreed to the appointment because they seem to have no motivation for changing anything or taking advantage of any solutions that suggest or want to provide.

They just want to look at your presentation or "pick your brain" for free. They might even do this more than once.

Clearly, they are not "willing" to make a decision, and no sale will ever happen — no matter how much they say they want or need to do something — before and until this challenge is met.

They might even be fooling themselves into thinking that they are capable of a decision when, in fact, they are not.

The "Able" Variable

Then there is "ABLE." This is the *financial* assessment or measurement.

The "able" test may be difficult for you to determine — depending on the scope, urgency, and total price of the project. It may have several variables involved.

People can *act* like they can afford what they tell you they want to spend or invest. They also can manipulate their loan application to keep from getting approved for credit as a way of delaying the project.

"Able" means that someone can pay cash for their purchase (quite common), they can make several installment payments (if that is how you are willing to work with them), it can be an insurance settlement or a grant, or they have the credit-worthiness or financial rating to secure a loan at a reasonable rate and terms to move forward with their purchasing decision.

It means that they can fund their purchase — through a variety of ways and possibilities, including personal savings, contributions from family members, health or accident insurance benefits, worker's comp insurance, a liability settlement, a home improvement loan, a home equity loan or line-of-credit, refinance, or other financial tools — and convey an initial deposit such as you are requesting to commence the work.

The "Able" Test

This test of being "able" depends on what you are selling (handyman services, simple remodeling, minor kitchen or bath makeovers, room additions, or major remodeling) how the sale is structured, the dollar amount of the sale, and the time it will take to complete the project.

If the sale is under $100, it should be a simple cash (check, credit or debit card, or purchase order) transaction. No muss, no fuss. If the cash isn't there or the credit card cannot be used for a relatively minor or incidental purchase (in terms of money), the "able" test fails.

If the sale is up to $1,000 or so, you may take an initial deposit with the purchase order and receive the final payment upon delivery or installation of your product — or commencement of your services. Maybe you'll decide to take installment payments.

For sales in the five-figures and up, there could be many payment options. It could be paid in full at the time of the order or sale. It could be a 50% deposit with the balance due upon delivery, installation, or commencement. You might use a draw schedule. You could do a percentage of completion.

For small amounts, the entire sum could be due upon invoice.

Perhaps, it's an initial deposit with two or more installments after that. It might be a direct bill to an insurance company, support group, or other agency.

Still, the entire financial commitment of the purchase must be dischargeable in some way by your potential client or customer — even if someone other your client is paying for the work — for this customer to be considered meeting the "able" test.

There Must Be Full Payment

Regardless of how the financial terms are arranged, your client or customer must be able to pay for what is being ordered to be considered "able."

Even if they are seeking bank financing or using a line of credit for their purchase, they still must be able to qualify for the funding and receive it to complete their transaction with you. Then they must have the financial resources on hand or in receivables to meet the repayment terms of the loan.

For even larger sales, the same guidelines apply whether financing, personal funds, or proceeds from settlements or insurance are used. They still a way of paying for their purchase.

Despite the size of the transaction, your customer or client (business or consumer) must be capable of making a decision on what you are providing by having the financial resources to tender any required initial deposit with their order or scope of services agreement. Then they need to be capable of paying the outstanding balance, or have the credit-worthiness to secure bank financing. All this is without anything else being a factor, such as selling any assets or waiting for funds.

This is how the "able" test is measured.

If the money is not there or payment in full cannot be assured, the purchase can't proceed and the "able" test will have failed.

Looks Can Be Deceiving

Looks can be deceiving. You can't tell just by looking whether someone is "able." You can't always tell just by looking at the company either. You can't always tell by asking either.

Stating what you expect as an initial deposit or asking a general question about their credit-worthiness may help you determine how "able" someone or some company is to make a decision to what you offer.

However, it's possible that they will just tell you what they think you want to hear — or not be able to answer your question without checking with someone else first. They may not have a realistic idea of the total expense.

Of course, a lot is going to depend on the size of the project and the financial or funding resources that might be available.

You can ask them a question about any issues that they think might affect their getting a loan or the required funds for the purchase of what you are proposing. You don't need to know the details — just if there are any.

If such issues exist, perhaps you have a lender you like or a resource you can suggest to them.

Remaining Objective

The powerful part about the "ready, willing, and able" test is that it is OBJECTIVE — if you allow it to be.

Without trying to add *shades* or degrees of whether someone is "ready" or "willing" or "able," this test is a straightforward, objective one.

Nevertheless, the interpretation of it and its actual application often means that many people are misjudged on their ability to make a buying decision.

As a result, some people are afforded too much attention and considered more qualified to make a decision than they really are — because of how they appear, the way they talk, or their particular situation that you happen to identify with.

The "Ready, Willing, And Able" Test

Sometimes just the interest people appear to show can make them seem more qualified than they really are.

Conversely, others who actually are capable of making a decision — and may have a more urgent need — may be ignored or pursued less diligently because of they you interact with them.

Your personal feelings about how "good" someone is cannot be allowed to enter into your rating. Feelings need to be shelved for rating purposes.

How well you like or dislike someone or their company — or whatever interests you may have in common with them — should have no bearing on the grade or mark you give them.

The key to the successful use of the "ready, willing, and able" test is to remain objective.

Getting Consistent Results

If the "ready, willing, and able" test is not applied objectively or evenly, you won't get a consistent rating or mark for your customers or sales leads, and your sales process — including your follow-up activity — will be less effective.

You need to know and be able to trust that whatever grade or mark that you apply or give to someone will immediately tell you — and any others on your team (such as managers, assistants, and associates) that might occasionally help you — what the likelihood is of them making a decision at any moment.

This is how you will strategize your time and efforts to work the most effectively and efficiently with the leads and customer base that you have — so that you can produce the sales that are the most likely and feasible.

Remember that someone either satisfies each of the three criteria completely or they don't.

There's no "partial" or "almost" to it. This is how the grading is applied.

It's easy to let someone's speech, appearance, status, position, apparent need, title, company, or actions influence how you treat them.

If someone is dressed neatly or groomed well, or polite or pleasant, there may be a tendency to treat them more credibly or to not question their abilities as much as you might with someone who looks or acts less likely to be ready to make a decision.

Similarly, if someone is in obvious need of a solution and you can empathize with their situation, this does not automatically translate to someone who can make an immediate decision to work with you.

The "Ready, Willing, And Able" Test

Putting It All Together

It doesn't matter how well you like someone or how well you interact with them while you are together with them in your office or their home or office — or even at you booth at a home show or fair.

You just need to ask yourself the ready, willing, and able questions for each person and answer them honestly.

No fudging — just an honest assessment. It really is that simple.

If someone can make a decision without their present physical situation being a factor, they are "ready."

They just need to be able to make a commitment without relying on completion of any improvements that are underway, selling anything to raise revenues, exhausting their current supplies or inventory, transitioning from existing products or services that yours will replace or augment, going through a bidding process, or getting the advice of their team or family about the appropriateness of a project.

If they are emotionally capable or prepared to make such a decision because they have identified a need or their current solution just doesn't meet their requirements any longer — or offer them the efficiency or technology they desire — then they are "willing."

Finally, if they have the financial or credit resources to move forward with making a purchasing decision, they are "able."

Put all three measurements together, and the customer, client, or sales lead you're working with has satisfied the "ready, willing, and able" test.

There is nothing mysterious or difficult about the "ready, willing, and able" test.

It is a set of objective criteria that will help you assess someone's ability to make a decision on the solutions, products, or services you are offering.

Keep personalities out of the equation and focus just on the facts.

Then you can allocate your time accordingly to work with those people who are the most likely to make a purchasing decision at the moment.

3

An "A" Rating Isn't Sufficient

Committing To A Rating System

If you've read this far, and you're not already using some type of a formal rating system, you really should begin doing so.

There's no time like right now to get started.

This is particularly true if you are serious about making more sales and keeping track of which customers or sales leads are in the best position to make a decision.

You need to be able to keep track of your customers and leads and identify which ones require your attention or your focus — and which ones need little or no attention.

The timesavings alone makes it worthwhile.

Then you can allocate your energy where it will do the most good — working with those who are the closest to making a decision as well as those who could be ready to make a decision soon — with a little coaching and encouragement from you.

Some salespeople and contractors just keep track of their best customers and sales leads in their head and don't worry too much about the rest of their customers.

Others make random notes about their customers but don't employ a formal way of rating customers or leads — or keeping track of the notes they've made.

Regardless of what you've been using so far for a rating system, keep an open mind as you read this chapter.

I've promised you a revolutionary, rating system, and by the end of this chapter, you'll see just how special it is.

It's a simple, yet powerful, system that will allow you to produce more sales (making you more money) and manage your time more effectively (saving wasted or unproductive activity).

Identifying Your Top Possibilities

Depending on how many people you see or talk with in a week's time, it may be easy to keep track of the one or two top customers without formally rating them.

But, are you sure just *how* good they are and that they are the only ones you should be focusing on?

It's easy to misjudge people and their interest level in an initial meeting or conversation. That's why an objective set of criteria are important, and that's why a formal rating system that uses such criteria is useful.

You can give someone an "A" rating or mark them "hot" based on what seemed to be their level of interest, and your "feeling" about them.

However, you really need to apply the "ready, willing, and able" test to verify that they are as good as you think they are and that you're not just *wishing* them into an "A" or top rating.

Using The "A-B-C" Rating System

Again, the basis of any quality rating system needs to be a set of objective criteria, and the "ready, willing, and able" test seems to meet our requirements.

Since you already may be using an "A-B-C" rating system (or a variation of it), let's discuss how to apply those grades or marks using the "ready, willing, and able" formula.

Keep in mind that even when something like this "ready, willing, and able" rating test is used, there often are wide variations in the results — due largely to the fact that the test may be only loosely applied and then used subjectively rather than objectively.

Using this "A-B-C" rating system, a customer or sales lead who is ready, willing, and able to make a decision on acquiring or using what you offer — with no conditions or contingencies applied to that decision — would be rated as an "**A**."

There should be absolutely no guesswork or "feeling" or interpretation about whether someone "deserves" an "A" rating.

Either someone satisfies all three of the tests or they don't. If they do, they're an "A." It's that simple.

However, if you are working with someone who is otherwise prepared to make a decision on your product or solution — and you use a financing contingency to help them start the paperwork — it's the same as not having any conditions, and the customer or sales lead still would be rated as an "A."

If *one* of the criteria has not been met or satisfied — such as not being sure what they actually want in a new product, design, general solution, or service, needing to complete some minor repairs or improvements first, wanting to "think about" what you've shown or discussed with them, not having the funds or resources available to commit to a decision, or just not having the authority to commit their household or company to a purchasing decision — a "**B**" would apply.

If *two or more* of the "ready, willing, and able" criteria are missing, those potential customers and clients, or sales leads, would be rated a "**C**."

Adding A "D" To The Rating System

People who are not seriously looking for a new product or solution or aren't capable of making a decision on acquiring or using it — as well as those who are not or will not be in a position to commit to your proposal — would be rated as a "**D**."

This specifically relates to what you sell — or what your competition offers or has access to that is similar to what you provide.

This could include those people or companies that do not have sufficient financial resources or revenue to qualify to purchase a product or design solution that you offer that reasonably meets their stated or observed needs, ones who need financing but can't get approved for it, those who recently remodeled their space and have no interest in replacing or supplementing the improvements in the foreseeable future, people moving out of their current home or leaving your area, those who have unrealistic expectations or demands, or those companies that are in the process of shutting down or merging with another.

However, using just the basic "A," "B," "C," and "D" grades are not SUFFICIENT for your purposes.

You won't get the total picture of your potential or existing customers or clients using just this system. Just adding more letter grades won't help either.

Adjusting Your Rating System

The "ready, willing, and able" test is fine as far as it goes, but there is one key component missing for a totally effective and efficient rating system.

You must know how well someone LIKES the idea of working with you and your company, what they think you can bring to the relationship, and the products or solutions you offer to their specified needs.

This one additional aspect of the rating makes all the difference in making a sale — and in apportioning your time.

It allows you to focus your efforts on identifying and working just with those people who like what you offer. They will be more likely to do business with you than those people who are indifferent or don't especially care for you, your company, or your products or services.

If people don't like what you are proposing or willing to offer them, or they don't feel that you can meet their needs, they are not likely to decide to work with you — no matter what you do or how hard you try.

Effort Is Not The Answer

Regardless of how many times you call, write, email, or text someone who has seen what you have shown them or heard about what you offer, if they don't like what you can do for them or don't care for your company, they are not going to work with you.

Simply put, what you bring to the table just doesn't work for them or satisfy their needs.

In cases like these, your effort has nothing to do with making a sale. In fact, how nice or professional you are, how often you contact or communicate with your customers or sales leads, what you are prepared to do for and with them, what you have shown them about your products or services, the quality and value of what you offer, or how hard you try will have little effect.

So while someone might truly be "ready, willing, and able," this determination just indicates that they are capable of making a decision to acquire a product or service like yours and likely will be able to do so quickly — certainly within 30 days (and possibly immediately or within a day or two).

However, without the "LIKEABILITY" factor being present, when such a decision is made to move forward, it will not involve you, your company, or specifically what you offer.

Introducing The "A-1" Rating

Finding someone who is prepared to make a decision on something you offer who satisfies the "ready, willing, and able" criteria is a great start.

However, you need to make sure that they want to work with you, that you can meet their needs with what you can show them, and that they like you before you can make the sale or get the order.

And, the way that you determine this is by *asking* and *listening*.

Then, you need to have a way of keeping track of those customers and sales leads who are "ready, willing, and able" to make a decision quickly on getting what you offer who also LIKE the idea of working with you.

This one distinction makes all the difference in your ratings — and ultimately in your sales efficiency.

Take an "A" customer that meets the "ready, willing, and able" criteria and then add the suffix "1" to their grade or mark if they like what you and your company offer and would like to work with you.

Now they become an *"A-1"* customer, client, or sales lead — the best chance you have for getting a purchasing decision at any given moment.

This one change will make an enormous difference in how you work with your sales leads and customer database, and you will be more effective and efficient.

Refining The Traditional Rating System

When you adopt the new, expanded rating system, you won't be eliminating the traditional "A," "B," "C," and "D" ratings.

You are just creating the additional, modified ratings of *"A-1," "B-1," "C-1,"* and *"D-1"* to refine and improve your rating system.

Thus, as you review your customer base and sales leads to formulate your contact strategy and approach for each customer, you now can choose to allocate your time and resources to maintain contact with just those customers or sales leads who have the highest probability of actually working with you to purchase or acquire what you offer — those you have given the additional designation of *"1"* after their letter grade.

This especially applies to those top customers who are capable of purchasing within the next 30 days (or less) — your newly defined "A-1" customers.

In addition to having a customer who is "ready, willing, and able" to make a decision quickly, you now can differentiate between an "A" (who is capable of a decision but isn't inclined to work with you) and an "A-1" customer or sales lead that *likes* you and what you offer well enough to want to work with you.

Furthermore, your "B," "C," and "D" customers who like you, your company, and what you offer well enough to want to work with you and make a purchasing decision will become *"B-1," "C-1,"* and *"D-1"* customers or sales leads, respectively.

Applying The "A-1" Rating Objectively

Just as it is with the "ready, willing, and able" test, you want to make sure that the test for the additional "1" rating or mark is objective and not subjective.

You can't invent "A-1" customers at will.

You can't wish someone into an "A-1" rating just because you want to make a sale or want to impress yourself, your company, or your associates with how many "A-1"s that you have.

You can't call someone who really is an "A" an "A-1" just because you like them or think they are a strong "A" — or because you think you need to have an "A-1" customer or sales lead to work with.

An "A" Rating Isn't Sufficient

You can't just use it to indicate that you think someone will make a decision quickly, and you can't use it because you want them to have what you offer. Remain objective throughout the rating process.

The "A-1" rating must only be used when all four attributes are present — ready, willing, able, *and* like — and not as a way of flagging or elevating an otherwise non-"A-1" customer.

Giving You An Edge With Your Time

This enhanced rating system that I am giving you provides an edge in planning how to organize your day and how you schedule your follow-up contact with your customers and sales leads.

You no longer need to pursue or concentrate on those people who aren't likely to work with you no matter how hard you try. They simply don't like your approach or don't think that you can meet their needs — and no amount of additional contact is going to change that.

Instead, you can devote your time and energies to working just with those customers who are the most likely to decide to use what you offer.

So, each day when you are deciding who you need to work with in the limited amount of time you have available, you should start with your "A-1" customers.

They require the most immediate attention, and because now you have clearly marked who they are, you can concentrate on working with them.

After that, you can move on to working with your top "B-1" and "C-1" customers to see what you can do to help them satisfy the issues keeping them from a decision and move them along to an "A-1" rating.

Under this plan, you won't be focusing on your "A," "B," and "C" customers, and you will have limited contact with them.

This is the revolutionary rating system that will allow you to produce more sales and save time.

Hoarding Isn't The Answer

Just having several top-ranked customers on file in your desk drawer or database because you feel good about them is not the way to make more sales.

Some salespeople rely on this so much that they actually have long lists or a big stack of cards of such customers.

They hoard what they believe to be their top customers — without doing anything to facilitate a decision.

They act as if these people always are going to be interested and ready to do something with them.

Regardless of whether these people have been correctly rated as someone who actually will make a decision, or just identified because of a "feeling," keeping a bunch of names on file with no action to support their high rating will only cause disappointment — and produce no sales.

In this scenario, everyone loses — you, your company, and your potential customers.

People Are Subject To Change

Keeping large stacks of cards or computer records on file of "good" customers who will "surely buy something someday" without reaching out to those people or maintaining regular contact with them is just wasting potential sales opportunities.

Such a policy assumes that people or their needs don't change over time, but obviously, they can and do.

An "A" or "A-1" customer from 6 months ago likely has already done something by now (especially if the rating was done correctly) — and keeping them on file as a potential sale is just wishful thinking.

An "A-1" *Is* Special

Using my new rating system, an "A-1" customer, sales lead, or potential client is the best one that you can work with or focus on at any particular time because they *like* you, they *like* what you offer better than or as well as anything else they have seen or considered, and they are *ready, willing, and able* to make a quick decision — and very probably with you.

However, it doesn't mean that this is automatic.

It still takes work because you'll be in competition with other estimators, remodelers, trade contractors, occupational therapists and other professionals that also appeal to your customers and can address their needs.

If you truly are grading, rating, or marking your customers and sales leads properly — using the *ready, willing, able,* and *like* criteria — you should have no more than one or two "A-1" customers or sales leads at any given time. This makes them very special.

On occasion, you might not have any "A-1"s, and that's OK — it's temporary.

If you have more than a couple of "A-1"s at any one time, you likely are not being diligent enough in your ratings or in pursuing the sale or transaction.

An "A-1" customer or sales lead is extremely important to you. However, you can't produce them at will or wish them into existence. Also, there is nothing automatic about making a sale to an "A-1."

The True "A-1" Customer

The true "A-1" customer or sales lead is in position to make a buying decision right now — on this appointment or contact that you're having with them.

Therefore, you are in a race against the clock with all the everyone else in your marketplace that also can meet their needs.

Time truly is of the essence.

There may not be another chance to make a sale or get a commitment from an "A-1" customer "tomorrow."

Make it today, if possible — on this appointment or conversation. At least get the commitment to proceed.

Enjoying Success With The "A-1"

You should have a very high closing rate with your "A-1" customers because of your commitment to them and the relationships that you are building with them.

If it's a sales lead that you haven't fully developed, but you know enough about them to rate them as an "A—1," you should still have a high degree of success with them.

Nothing is automatic, but if the sale seems imminent while you're talking with them or showing them what you have to offer, don't put off asking for the sale until a later meeting or conversation.

You may not get another chance to close the sale or transaction with those customers or sales leads.

Don't risk losing a sale to anyone else.

Your "A-1" customers are your best chance for sales success at any moment.

Special Contact For Your "A"s

In addition to your normal written and telephone post-visit contact that you conduct with everyone you meet, one more step is necessary for just your "A" customers — not your "A-1"s or any other ratings.

The presumption is that that these "A" rated customers already decided to do business with someone else and bought from them — that's why you rated them an "A."

Wait until 30 days or so have elapsed since your initial meeting or conversation with them, and then telephone just your "A" sales leads again to learn what they bought or decided on — and to discuss it with them.

However, if they didn't choose another company and still want to acquire something like you offer to meet their needs or address their issues, evaluate why they have not made a decision and re-grade them accordingly.

You still might be able to work with them.

Adding Your Congratulations

When you talk with your "A" customers or sales leads and they have made a decision on something else, you'll have an opportunity to congratulate them and determine why they selected what they did and how they think it will meet their needs.

This is an important gesture and will differentiate you from your competition.

Be sincere in your congratulations and earnest in learning why they chose what they did. Try to find out how it differs from what you might have shown, offered, or discussed with them.

Also, be sure to send them a congratulations card or email. This should be professional and sincere as well.

There should be no expression of disappointment since you knew when you met or spoke with them that you and your company didn't quite hit it off with them.

Simply tell them that you enjoyed getting to know them and offer your assistance for them or any of their friends or colleagues should they need it.

An "A" customer may seem like a "lost sale" because they worked with someone else, but you weren't seriously in the running for their business.

By expressing a sincere happiness for their decision, you will create goodwill and a potential ambassador that can produce future referrals.

Focusing On Your "A"s Again

If you learn from talking with your "A" customers or sales leads, when you call them a month after your initial conversation or meeting, that they haven't made a decision because their timing or expectations changed — or that they really weren't "ready, willing, and able" after all — re-mark them to what seems appropriate.

They might be interested in working with you (which would add a "1" to their new, revised mark).

It's quite possible that their expectations changed and now your approach seems more reasonable to them.

If they decided to employ a temporary, interim solution for their needs, learn when they would like to move forward on a more permanent or more effective solution and plan on talking with them a couple of times prior to then to find out how you can help them or what information you can furnish to assist them in making their ultimate decision.

Rating With All Four Factors

To be an "A-1" customer, sales lead, or potential client, all four tests must be satisfied: ready, willing, able, *and* like.

This is the only rating where the answers to all four questions will be — and must be — "Yes."

The other ratings ("A," "B," "B-1," "C," "C-1," "D," and "D-1") are directly dependent on the objective answers to these four questions or tests as well — and reflect that at least one of the answers is "*No.*"

Also, be careful not to misrank someone because you are not establishing a good rapport with them, or they don't like what you offer or your approach to solving their issues — especially if they are someone who appears to be serious about making a decision.

An "A" customer or sales lead who is ready, willing, and able to make a decision on a product or solution such as you offer but does not like your approach or who needs something significantly different than what you can show them may well go someplace else or talk to another company within a few days (or even later that same day) and make a decision with someone else.

Don't lose track of the "D" rated people. Many salespeople, managers, and business owners have a tendency to not include a "D" in their ratings because they are impatient or unable to address their needs.

Ignoring or not counting the "D"s is not correct and will lead to an inaccurate analysis of your lead generation history and quality. Including them provides opportunities for an eventual sale that you might uncover in your post-visit follow-up contact.

Begin adding the "1" rating to the appropriate letter mark to denote those customers who like you, your company, and your approach to their issues — and focus your time and efforts on helping them to reach their decisions.

This is the real power of this rating system.

You will become more effective, efficient, and productive as a result.

4

Going Behind The Mark

Knowing The Rating Possibilities

As we just discussed in the previous chapter, there are eight possible ratings or marks that you will use to initially categorize someone's level of interest in purchasing what you offer or in working with you.

This rating is subject to change as you learn more about your customers and leads and how you might be able to work them, but this is where the assessment begins.

The rating or marking is based on applying the "ready," "willing," and "able" test to your customers and then using the new test with the suffix "1" that I have given you for indicating "like" when it applies.

Four of the marks show a general interest.

Four indicate a preference for working with you and your company.

The four *general interest* ratings are "A," "B," "C," and "D." These scores, grades, rankings, marks, or ratings denote various levels of interest and ability to act but do not signify that they want to do business with you.

The four *specific interest* ratings that you'll use to indicate that people are inclined to work with you to buy what you offer are "A-1," "B-1," "C-1," and "D-1." These scores, grades, rankings, marks, or ratings also denote various levels of interest and ability to act, but they signify that people are willing to do business with you.

Applying The "A" Mark

Through a series of various discovery questions, you can help yourself determine your customer's mark or rating.

You are attempting to measure three variables — "ready," "willing," and "able." When you are satisfied that *all three* of these have been met, you have an "A" customer.

This means no conditions, no contingencies, and no hedging. They know what they want and are ready to make a decision immediately to purchase, but it could take up to a month or so for them to do so.

An "A" customer (1) does not have anything to complete or get ready before you can begin your work — or anything to put out for bids or receive second opinions on the work to be done before making a decision, **and**

(2) is emotionally or psychologically ready to make a decision and select a product or solution for their current needs because what they have now just isn't accomplishing what they need and they are tired of coping with it — or they are ready to expand and augment what they have, **and**

(3) has the cash (from savings or family contributions), credit card, purchase order, line-of-credit, bank loan, or funds promised or available for their purchase, including an initial deposit, if required.

Applying The "A-1" Mark

Here again, you are attempting to measure three variables — "ready," "willing," and "able." However, you also are looking for and evaluating the presence of that all-important fourth variable.

You will be determining if "like" has been met. Then, when you are satisfied that all four of these questions have been answered, you have an "A-1" customer.

This means no physical conditions or other factors prevent making a decision or proceeding with you.

That decision could be imminent.

An **"A-1"** customer (1) does not have to complete any other improvements, get things ready, gets bids, or receive approval from others before making a decision, **and**

(2) is emotionally or psychologically ready to make a decision and select a product or solution for their current needs because what they have now just isn't accomplishing what they need and they are tired of coping with it — or they are ready to expand and augment what they have, **and**

(3) has the cash (from savings or family contributions), credit card, purchase order, line-of-credit, bank loan, or funds promised or available for their purchase, including an initial deposit, if required, **and**

(4) likes working with you and your company, likes your approach to their situation, likes what you have outlined that you can offer them, likes your actual proposal — and feels that their needs can be met by purchasing what you offer.

It doesn't mean that the "A-1" customer or sales lead is an automatic sale or transaction, but this is where you are going to find your sales — you have as good a chance, or even a better one, than other companies to compete for and sign these customers.

This is your optimum customer because they have the capacity and interest to make a decision.

Applying The "B" Mark

The "B" mark results when one, *and only one*, of the "ready," "willing," and "able" components is missing. It can be any of the three, but typically, it is the "willing" test that is missing — as in waiting to make a decision that seems like it should be easy to make, given the facts.

A "B" customer (1) may be waiting to complete some minor repairs or improvements, gets bids, or receive the approval of others before making a decision, **or**

(2) may not be emotionally or psychologically ready to make a decision because they want time to think about what they are contemplating, need to get the advice of others, aren't sure what they want to do, haven't set a budget, or aren't totally committed to making the decision, **or**

(3) may not have the funds available to tender an initial deposit or complete installment payments from cash on hand or revenues, and may not have the ability to obtain financing to move forward on the purchase or acquisition of what you offer.

Remember it's just *one* of those variables to which the answer is "no." The answer to the other two is "yes."

It doesn't matter which one of the three is missing, and it won't necessarily be the same factor that is missing for each "B" customer or sales lead.

This often means that a month or more — sometimes even up to six months or longer — might be required to accomplish or eliminate the missing variable.

Applying The "B-1" Mark

Here, you are looking for the "like" factor. It will be present even though *one* of the other vital tests will be missing. This results in a score or rating of a "B-1."

Typically, it is the "willing" test that is going to be missing — showing up as a reluctance to make a decision that seems like it should be easy to make.

A **"B-1"** customer (1) may waiting to complete some minor repairs or improvements, gets bids, or receive approval from others first, **or**

(2) may not be emotionally or psychologically ready to make a decision to move forward because they want time to think about what they are contemplating, aren't sure what they want to do, or aren't totally committed to making the decision, **or**

(3) may not have the funds available for an initial deposit, if required, or the ability to complete

installment payments from cash on hand or revenues, and may not be able to obtain financing to move forward with the project you offer, **but**

(4) likes you and your company and what you can offer them well enough to want to work with you as you help them work through or resolve the situation that is preventing them from making a decision, and in turn, allow them to become an "A-1."

Remember that it's just *one* of these variables to which the answer is "no." The answer to the others — including "like" — is "yes."

It's just determining which one is missing and then working to alleviate that deficiency.

This often means that a month or more — sometimes even up to six months or longer — might be required to accomplish the missing variable.

Applying The "C" Mark

When at least two (even all three) of the variables have not been satisfied — but there still is some interest in purchasing the type of solution you are discussing with them, you have a rating or mark of a "C."

The "C" means that any combination of the rating or measurement factors have yet to be satisfied, such as "ready" and "willing," "ready" and "able," "willing" and "able," or all three of them.

A "**C**" customer (1) may need to complete some minor repairs or improvements, gets bids, or receive the approval of others before making a decision, **and/or**

(2) likely will not be emotionally or psychologically ready to make a decision because they want time to think about what they are contemplating — or they are not totally committed to making the decision or sure of what they want to do, **and/or**

(3) possibly may not have the funds available to tender an initial deposit, if you require it, or complete the financial arrangement.

Here, it's at least *two* of those variables to which the answer is "no" — and it could even be all three.

It doesn't matter which variables are missing, but such a person is far away from a decision until those issues are resolved.

This often means that several months to a year or more might be required before such a customer has accomplished all of the required tests.

With the "C," it's not uncommon for a decision to never happen.

Applying The "C-1" Mark

The big difference between the "C" and the "C-1" is the presence of the "like" factor. Your customer still has two or even all three of the "ready-willing-and-able" variables to satisfy, but the "like" variable is in place. Thus, you have a mark or rating of a "C-1."

Like the "C" rating or mark, the "C-1" means that "ready" and "willing," "ready" and "able," or "willing" and "able" — and possibly all three of them — are missing. However, now the "like" variable is present.

A **"C-1"** customer (1) may need to complete some minor repairs or improvements, gets bids, or receive the approval of others before making a decision, **and/or**

(2) likely will not be emotionally or psychologically ready to make a decision because they want time to think about what they are contemplating — or they are not totally committed to making the decision or sure of what they want to do, **and/or**

(3) may not have the funds available to tender an initial deposit, if you require it, or complete the financial arrangement, **but**

(4) likes you personally and likes what you and your company can offer well enough to want to work with you as you help work through the two or three missing

conditions that need to be satisfied first before they can make a decision.

At least *two* of those variables — and possibly all three of the "ready, willing, and able" ones — will be answered "no," but the "like" factor will be answered "yes."

It doesn't matter which variables are missing, but such a person or company is far away from a decision until those issues are resolved.

This often means that several months to a year or more might be required before such a customer has accomplished all of the required tests.

Applying The "D" Mark

A "D" mark means that no decision is possible for at least a year — and maybe not even then. There are many factors that result in a "D" mark, but all stem from the fact that *all three variables* cannot be met or satisfied.

A "D" customer (1) must wait until some physical repair or other requirement is satisfied or made ready before committing to a decision, **and**

(2) is not emotionally or psychologically ready to make a decision because they recently completed some other type of improvement and have to live or work with it

first, feel that they cannot make the changes they want with what they are willing or able to invest in other solutions, may consider moving out of your area, or have no interest or intention of doing anything, **and**

(3) does not have the funds, cash flow, or financial ability for an initial deposit or installment payments and cannot qualify for financing now or in the foreseeable future for the purchase or acquisition of what you offer.

They might have other conditions as well such as large medical bills, financial judgments, pending lawsuits, student loans, late payments, repossessions, defaults, foreclosures; bankruptcies; loss of a job; failed business; or not being established in the area.

Applying The "D-1" Mark

A "D-1" mark still means that no decision is possible for at least a year. However, it also means that they like you well enough to consider doing business with you — when and if that ever becomes possible.

A "D-1" customer (1) must wait until some physical repair or other requirement is satisfied or made ready before committing to a decision, **and**

(2) is not emotionally or psychologically ready to make a decision because they recently completed some other type of improvement and have to live or work with it

first, entered into a contract for at least a year, feel that they cannot make the changes they want with what they are willing or able to invest in other solutions, may consider moving out of your area, or have no interest or intention of doing anything, **and**

(3) does not have the funds, cash flow, or financial ability for an initial deposit or installment payments and cannot qualify for financing for the purchase, lease, project, or acquisition of what you offer.

They might have other conditions as well such as large medical bills, financial judgment, pending lawsuits, student loans, late payments, repossessions, defaults, foreclosures, bankruptcies; unemployment, failed business; or not being established in the area, **and**

(4) likes you personally and likes what you and your company can offer them well enough to want to work with you as you help them work through all of the conditions that need to be satisfied and alleviated before they can consider making a decision.

They generally like your approach to being able to help them resolve their situation.

At-A-Glance Marking Summary

"A" Ready to make a decision, AND
     Willing to make a decision, AND

Going Behind The Mark

>
> Able to make a decision, AND
> Usually done very quickly — less than 30 days.

"A-1" Ready to make a decision, AND
Willing to make a decision, AND
Able to make a decision, AND
Likes working with you, AND
Usually done very quickly — less than 30 days.

"B" Ready and Willing, **but not** Able, OR
Willing and Able, **but not** Ready, OR
Able and Ready, **but not** Willing, AND
Often take 30-90 days — and as much as 180, or even longer, depending on what you sell.

"B-1" Ready and Willing, **but not** Able, OR
Willing and Able, **but not** Ready, OR
Able and Ready, **but not** Willing, AND
Likes working with you, AND
Often take 30-90 days — and as much as 180, or even longer, depending on what you sell.

"C" Ready, **but not** Willing, **and not** Able, OR
Willing, **but not** Able, **and not** Ready, OR
Able, **but not** Ready, **and not** Willing, OR
Not Ready, **not** Willing, **and not** Able, AND
Typically takes 90-365 days, or more.

"C-1" Ready, **but not** Willing, **and not** Able, OR
Willing, **but not** Able, **and not** Ready, OR

Able, **but not** Ready, **and not** Willing, OR
Not Ready, **not** Willing, **and not** Able, AND
Likes working with you, AND
Typically takes 90-365 days, or more.

"D" **Not** Ready, **not** Willing, **and not** Able, AND
Requires over a year, if ever, for a decision.

"D-1" **Not** Ready, **not** Willing, **and not** Able, AND
Likes working with you, AND
Requires over a year, if ever, for a decision.

5

Only A Few Can Be An "A-1"

The Importance Of Your "A-1"s

The most important people for you to be concentrating on each day are your "A-1" customers or sales leads, but of course not everyone can be an "A-1."

In fact, very few are or ever will be.

As I stressed in the previous chapter, you might have only one or two "A-1" customers at any given time. You might have none.

That's why your "A-1" customers are so special, and that's why you need to focus on getting a decision from as many of them as possible.

Strive for at least a 50% conversion ratio of your "A-1"s — that's getting a sale or transaction from at least half.

However, it's not important how many "A-1" customers you have at any one time (as long as you have some throughout the year).

It's only important that you know what to do with them to maximize the possibility of making a sale.

You can't — and must not — manufacture "A-1"s by giving this designation to someone who doesn't deserve it, based on the set of four objective criteria.

Either someone is an "A-1" or they are not.

Remember that an "A-1" designation does not mean that someone *will* buy with you — just that they can and that they might. Much is still up to you.

You are in competition for their business with other remodelers, handymen, and contractors in your market that also can satisfy their needs — and you can't leave anything to chance.

You Need To Be Intentional

As important as your "A-1" customers and leads are for your sales success, you can't count on them just contacting you when they are ready to make a decision.

You can't wait until they figure out on their own that you have shown them the correct solution or strategy.

If you wait for an "A-1" just to contact you on their own, you're going to lose out.

You have to intentionally schedule all contacts after the initial meeting, know why you are scheduling it, and know what you want to accomplish.

You have to take responsibility for your customer base and schedule the appropriate next contact with each of your customers.

The rating system helps here because it allows you to focus on those most likely to make a decision in the near-term and lets you maintain less intense and less frequent contact with those whose decision is farther away.

Contact Other Than Face-To-Face

While most salespeople feel that they need to schedule another appointment with each customer or sales lead after the initial contact or presentation, this idea is largely misunderstood.

It's true that you should use one appointment or contact to set the next one, but it doesn't necessarily — and usually doesn't — mean that another in-person visit or appointment in your office or their home or business location is required unless a sale is imminent or otherwise warranted.

There are so many other types of contacts that typically are more appropriate for the majority of your customers and sales leads than the physical, face-to-face meeting — because so few of them will be an "A-1."

I'm talking about emails, letters, notecards, postcards, and phone calls for the majority of your customers.

Over time, your frequency of contact will adjust according to the rating of your customers and leads — and how soon they are willing to act.

However, for those people that you do need to see again relatively soon (such as your "A-1"s or those you need to work with some more before determining where they are in the process), you must intentionally schedule a return appointment or contact and not just leave it up to them.

For some of your customers or leads you will have virtually no additional contact with them — or only an occasional telephone, email, or written contact.

For others, such as your "A-1" customers, your contact will be immediate and almost daily until you get the agreement agreed to and signed.

That's why this rating system is so powerful. It lets you identify and concentrate on just those people who are close to making a decision — and not just any decision but one that involves you and your company.

Working Efficiently

If you were to devote the same amount of time, effort, and energy to all of your customers or the people you talk with about buying or using what you offer — regardless of their interest level or ability to make a decision — you would have very little to show for your work.

Many people will never use you or your company to satisfy their expressed needs no matter what you do or say, and many others will never buy from you although they say they like working with you.

Spending an inordinate amount of time working with people that are not in a position to make a decision to acquire what you offer — or have no interest in doing so — will produce no tangible results.

You must not confuse activity for progress.

Your contact with your customers and sales leads needs to be at a frequency and of a type — and with a message — that is appropriate for their level of interest, timing, and ability (and willingness) to make a decision.

So while you devote everything you can within a very short period of time — literally hours or days — to help your "A-1" customers decide that you are the most appropriate choice for them, what about the vast majority of your traffic that is not rated as "A-1"?

Most of your traffic will be something other than an "A-1" — and most will never reach that "A-1" level.

However, if you did nothing with your customer base or sales leads except wait for the one or two "A-1"s to come along or materialize every couple of weeks, you would be missing out on so much and doing a disservice to you, your company, and your customers.

So for starters, you must be reasonably certain of the ability of each customer or sales lead to make a decision and how likely that is to include you.

This will allow you to identify the occasional "A-1" and to work effectively and efficiently with the rest of your customer base and sales leads.

However, this may not be so apparent on the initial appointment or outing.

Initial Post-Visit Contact

Start by sending everyone — and not just the "good" ones — a *handwritten* thank-you note (in your hand, not from an assistant or computer-generated) within the initial 24-hours following their meeting with you. In some cases, an email is appropriate to use.

Every message can be identical, and the notes, cards, or emails can be prepared in advance.

Essentially, you just need to say three things in your note or email message, and that is all. Thank them for contacting you, tell them you appreciate their time and interest in what you have to offer, and say that you look forward to working with them.

For a meeting in their home or office, or your office or showroom: "Thank you for meeting with me today. I appreciate your time and your interest in what we have to offer. I look forward to working with you."

For an email or telephone contact to you (if you get an actual mailing address that you can use): "Thank you for contacting me today. I appreciate your interest in what we have to offer, and I look forward to being able to help you (talking with you more about how we can help you)."

For a trade show booth or similar display: "Thank you for visiting us (our booth/display) today. I appreciate your interest in what we have to offer, and I look forward to being able to help you (talking with you more about how we can help you)."

This is why all the notes can be the same — with the only variation being where you meet with your customers or sales leads or how they contacted you.

Save the personalized message for later after you have begun to develop more of a relationship.

Then, after the notes have been sent, telephone everyone within a few days of your visit with them — beginning with the highest rated ones first and then progressing through all of your customers and leads.

For best results, establish a specific day or time to call them — and why you want the next contact (answer questions, share more information, clarify some of the details) before you conclude your initial presentation or conversation with them.

The call could even be the same day as the visit if that's what you've scheduled.

Verifying Your Initial Rating

Your post-visit phone call serves many purposes.

The first thing you do is thank them for contacting you or letting you meet with them.

Then, you can answer questions, verify and supplement information you received during the initial meeting or conversation, and establish the next contact.

Primarily though you are testing your rating or mark.

This is why you telephone *everyone* who has visited you — to make reasonably sure that you have marked them correctly and that you can proceed accordingly.

It's also why you do it reasonably soon after the initial contact because this lets you determine the course of your post-visit contact from that point.

An Exception To The Rule

The only exception to this calling plan is when you are reasonably certain that your rating of a "D" (and not "D-1") is correct and you find little positive value to be gained through additional contact.

For instance, when someone visits your trade show booth or showroom or otherwise contacts you and makes it very clear that they don't live in your area and wouldn't consider actually doing business with you because of that — or that they are planning to move out of your area to another locale — there is little to be achieved by telephoning them.

The same would be true for someone who calls you or contacts you through an ad, a social media site, or your website and clearly is not really looking for what you offer but just curious — maybe it's a neighbor, a shopper, or someone with just a general curiosity.

From what you learn during your initial conversation, you know that they are a "D" (again, not a "D-1") and your post-visit call — if you could even successfully contact them — would only verify what they told you and would not be a good use of your time.

They probably don't want to hear from you since they had no interest in what you offer when they contacted you or visited your display or showroom, and you have nothing to accomplish by talking with them — unless it's just to thank them for visiting and meeting with you or to explore the possibility of them giving you a referral.

Nevertheless, don't use the "D" rating unless it really applies, and don't use this line of thinking to avoid calling people as you should.

Amending The Rating

If it appears — even after your follow-up phone call with your customers or sales leads — that you will not be able to satisfy their needs, give them the appropriate letter mark without the "1" following it and move on to more interested people.

However, your telephone conversation with someone that appeared to be an "A," "B," or "C" while you were meeting or talking with them in their home or office, at your display, showroom, or office, or when they called you, may change your opinion about them.

They may reveal additional information that suggests that they actually do want to work with you and that their expectations are realistic. Then, you can amend their mark to an "A-1," "B-1," or "C-1" — and maintain contact accordingly.

In some cases, you may not get a chance to meet with someone very long or determine their actual rating with any degree of certainty during your initial meeting or conversation, and you will have to rely on this post-visit telephone call to make your assessment.

This is precisely why the post-visit phone call is used.

A "C-1" is a good *default rating* when you have nothing more to go on during an initial meeting or phone call.

Scheduling Your Time

You need to make sure that you are working with and maintaining contact with those people who like you and your company and your approach to helping them well enough to eventually decide to purchase what you offer as a solution to the needs they have expressed.

While we say that an "A" or "A-1" customer will make a decision within 30 days (and usually considerably less than that) to indicate how serious they are about making a decision, there are no similar timing parameters or suggestions that apply to the "B" or "B-1" and "C" or "C-1" customers.

It can take months or even years before some people are ready to make a decision, and some people will never be ready. That is one of the great benefits of this rating system — it allows you to determine and note how serious people are about moving forward with a decision and lets you schedule your time and contact strategies accordingly to focus on the most serious ones first.

Maintaining Your Focus

During your post-visit follow-up contact with your "B-1" and "C-1" customers and sales leads, your focus needs to be identifying what issues they have that are preventing a decision — such as fear of going ahead, price, or you.

Then you want to determine what it will take to remove those barriers to a decision — and how you can help this become a reality.

Normally, there is a ranking progression for customers and sales leads who have conditions or issues that need to be met or satisfied before they can make a decision.

For instance, a "C-1" customer will progress to a "B-1" customer and then ultimately to an "A-1" customer as they become more serious about acquiring what you offer — or they solve or eliminate some of the issues and conditions that have prevented or forestalled a decision previously.

However, a "C-1" customer can skip the "B-1" step altogether and go straight to being an "A-1" if the barriers or conditions that had existed as a "C-1" have disappeared.

Even some of your "D-1" customers can work through the conditions that prevented them from being able to make a decision, and you can help make that happen.

So does every "C-1" customer or sales lead move up to being a "B-1" customer? Does every "B-1" customer move to an "A-1"? Of course not. There is nothing that certain in sales.

Even if someone moves up to an "A-1" or starts out there, not every "A-1" will purchase with you either. However, that shouldn't stop you from trying to capitalize on each customer or sales lead to get the greatest return possible — with the goal of getting *at least* half of your "A-1"s to choose to work with you.

You'll Only Close An "A-1"

As you maintain contact with each customer or sales lead, you are searching for what it will take to get them to an "A-1" mark or rating so that you can create a serious interest in what you are offering them and get them to make a decision to work with you.

Not everyone will transition from a lower grade or mark to an "A-1."

Some people will start out as a "C-1" or "D-1" and will always be a "C-1" or "D-1." No sale will ever occur with these people — no matter how hard you work.

You will only get a decision to move forward with an "A-1" customer — even if they literally turn into one while you're talking with them (because the prior conditions or issues that prevented them from making a decision have disappeared).

This is a key concept — only an "A-1" customer will ever make a decision, regardless of what their mark or rating was when you started the conversation or appointment.

You Can't Force It

By definition, a "B-1" customer can't make a decision.

They have one of the "ready, willing, and able" criteria to satisfy. The likeability factor is there but one of the other elements impacting their decision is missing.

The same is true of a "C-1" — with at least two of the defining criteria missing.

With a "D-1," all of the criteria for making a decision are missing.

Some people will be a "C-1" on their initial contact with you and will still be a "C-1" two years later.

You won't get a decision from everyone, and you can't force someone to change from a lower grade to an "A-1" if they really aren't ready, willing, or able to make a decision. Some people will never be able to commit to making a decision or changing what they have.

Just be aware of the opportunities and changes in someone's personal situation that might indicate an ability to make a decision that previously was not present.

People's Situations Can Change

Just as some people will remain a "C-1" for months or even years after you meet them, others will change — sometimes between contacts with them — as their needs, requirements, and timing evolve.

In the case of progressive based conditions, obviously the needs will change over time.

While you'd like for people to change from a "C-1" to a "B-1" or even an "A-1," the change — when it occurs — won't always be in a positive direction.

Some people will move away from a decision rather than toward it, and their grade or mark will reflect that change as well.

One of the principal changes can be financial. In the case of consumers, it could be a change in employment or some type of family or medical emergency that taps into their financial resources. It also could be a traumatic medical situation that demands a more urgent response than previously discussed or considered.

Household sizes can change as babies are born, adult children move back in, and divorces occur.

Also, the way that they feel about working with you or what you're showing them can change — what they liked or didn't care for previously can now be very different.

For businesses, there are many dynamics that could affect a decision, including cash flow, management, and direction.

Only a few people can be an "A-1" customer or sales lead at any one time — and some of your customers may never move up from their initial grade or mark to that next higher rating.

Nevertheless, you need to be committed to monitoring all of your customers or sales leads for changes in their personal and economic situations that will move them closer to (or occasionally even further away from) the time when they can make a decision with you.

6

Don't Discount The "D"s

What A "D" Rating Means

In most cases, a "D" rating or mark does not represent "discard" or "don't bother" or "don't waste your time."

It is not a rating that is used when you can't think of anything else to use — it is not a "default" mark.

It is not a rating that you give to an otherwise "A" customer who simply doesn't like you or what you offer — or doesn't want to work with you.

It's not a rating or mark that you give to someone that you don't like or don't want to get to know because of your initial impressions.

While many salespeople think that a "D" customer or sales lead is a total waste of their time, the fact is that some people who visit your showroom, office, or display, or otherwise contact you, truly aren't in a position to make a decision on anything at that time — or at any time in the foreseeable or even distant future.

When I use a "D" rating, I generally figure on at least a year before someone is capable of making a decision.

A "D" Customer Is Not "Able"

With a "D" customer or sales lead, this is not a case of someone just not "willing" to make a decision but rather a general inability to make a decision — even if they really would like to do so.

Mostly, we're talking about not being "able" for financial reasons to make a decision until the passage of time has allowed someone to rectify some of the issues that prevent a more timely decision.

This is different from someone who says that it will be at least a year or more before they are interested in making or considering a decision ("willing").

Reasons For A "D" Rating

There are several reasons why someone might be rated a "D" — and none of them are because it's a "default" mark or rating when nothing else is known about them or when that person is not likeable or pleasant.

Don't Discount The "D"s

People may have credit or financial issues because of poor payment histories, large credit card or credit line balances, foreclosures, or repossessions. Perhaps they haven't established themselves in a new job or area well enough to be considered credit-worthy.

They could have extremely large, unexpected medical expenses.

Their credit score may be lower than any lender will use, their household income is too low to qualify for even the most liberal of terms for what they are seeking.

Businesses may be in a similar position.

However, money might not be the issue. In fact, qualifying for a loan may have nothing to do with it.

Some people are "professional lookers" — always looking but never buying. They never find anything they like because they don't intend to do anything different.

They cannot be regarded as potentially serious buyers.

In fact, you may wonder why such people even bother to make the effort to have you talk with them or show them potential solutions because they clearly have no intention of acting on anything.

Some of your customers and sales leads may include

people who have recently purchased or committed to a similar product or service or started renovations with someone else.

They will tell you that they are *"looking for ideas"* or just continuing to explore the market to *"see what else is available (out there)"* or *"making sure we didn't miss anything"* — or they may not tell you until later that they've already purchased something.

Such individuals are committed to their current homes or businesses and do not foresee any additional physical improvements or other types of changes. They clearly fail the "ready, willing, and able" test.

There could a medical emergency or a chronic health condition of a family member or key employee that might prevent someone from making a decision for an indefinite period of time until more is known about how to cope.

Keeping It In Perspective

It's important in working with a "D" customer or sales lead to remain objective — particularly about financial issues.

In such cases, a desire to do something different, such as acquire or purchase what you are offering — no matter how strong it is — cannot outweigh the facts at hand.

You may empathize — even sympathize — with this situation or condition, but that won't help them to be able to purchase anything with you.

The financial, previous commitment, medical, credit, or other conditions that someone might have do not allow a decision for the foreseeable future.

No matter how much you might like someone or want them to have what you offer, the facts speak for themselves.

You just need to be patient until the issues resulting in the "D" rating can be addressed or resolved.

A "D" Rating Can Change

A "D" rating does not mean necessarily that this condition is permanent!

This is a very important concept.

Just because you are assigning a "D" rating or mark to someone — for the basic reason that they are not able to make a decision — does not mean that they'll never be in a position to purchase something such as you offer. So don't throw their name away and forget about them.

It may take months or years for it to change, but there is a possibility that a person currently in this position may someday be able to make a purchasing decision with someone — possibly you.

What if someone's condition actually does change in the next several months or years?

Are you still going to be in the same business or selling your products or services in a few years? I'd like to think that you are.

When The "D" Rating Changes

So, the "D" rating isn't necessarily permanent and can change to something that signifies a greater willingness or ability to make a buying decision.

The question, then, is do you think that someone who used to be a "D" — because they were not able to qualify to purchase something such as you offer or because they had personal, business, or family issues that prevented even considering a decision at that time — might appreciate working with someone (such as you) who treated them with respect during that period of a year or more rather than appearing as though it was a waste of their time?

But, what if their condition does not change? What have you lost by being nice to someone and maintaining a little contact with them over the course of several months — except possibly a little time?

What does it really cost for you to be pleasant and professional to someone — even if they never acquire anything from with you?

What if their financial condition doesn't improve?

What if they don't decide to make any additional improvements or changes in the future?

What if they go out of business or leave the area?

Those are definite possibilities.

On the other hand, just a little of your time to maintain contact with your "D" customers may lead to a future sale when their condition changes.

Even without a sale, you'll likely create a positive word-of-mouth ambassador — and referrals are possible as well.

"D" Actually Means "D-1"

So far in this chapter, I have been talking about the "D" rating or mark as applying to anyone who is incapable of making a decision or qualifying for financing for more than a year — for financial, family, business climate, health, or other reasons.

That's only part of the story.

You have to add in the *likeability* factor in order to have some chance of a return on your investment.

Thus, when I talk about the possibilities of a "D" customer or sales lead having some value to you, I'm not talking about just anyone who is unwilling or uninterested in *ever* making a decision but someone who might eventually make a decision involving *you*.

I'm not suggesting that you maintain contact and stay connected with someone who can't or won't make a decision for over a year who doesn't at least like working with you and the possibility of using what you offer.

Therefore, in this chapter, whenever I mention or talk about the "D" customers or sales leads, I'm actually referring to the *"D-1"* customers.

The "D-1" is someone who has issues to overcome that will take at least a year — or more — to resolve, but they like you and what you offer well enough to want to work with you, when and if that time comes.

Your "D-1" customers and sales leads are people you can invest a little time in because of the possibility that a purchasing decision will eventually happen.

They are worth maintaining occasional contact with over time to monitor their progress and help them to feel good about you and your company.

Looking At The Bigger Picture

Other salespeople and businesses might not see the potential value in working with a "D-1" customer and dismiss or discount them as being unworthy of their time or energy.

They likely would not be willing to invest very much time in these customers or make a very meaningful presentation to them — or consider them for referrals or as potential word-of-mouth ambassadors.

In short, other salespeople and businesses would essentially consider a "D-1" customer to be a waste of their time.

While they would only be looking for the more obvious sales possibilities, you understand the larger picture.

You have the ability to see and interpret the condition that prevents a person from making a decision in the near-term as one that very well may be temporary.

Obviously, you would not spend time making a lengthy presentation with lesser-qualified or uninterested people at the expense of ignoring or minimizing other, more qualified customers or sales leads.

Nevertheless, even a brief encounter with a "D-1" customer or sales lead can be polite, pleasant, and professional if you want it to be — and it will make an impression on such a customer.

Being Strategic With Your "D-1"s

Just think of the advantage you'll have over the other salespeople and companies that weren't as professional, considerate, or kind — or as far-sighted — to the "D-1"s as you.

Remember what the potential value of the "D-1" customer or sales lead is to you and your company in terms of sharing your message and kindness with others and the relative ease of maintaining contact with such customers or sales leads over the course of the coming year or years — until such time as they might be able to make a decision.

Of course, some of the people who are rated a "D-1" will never change from the conditions or issues that are preventing a buying decision to be in a position where one is possible — with you or anyone else. Their economic or personal situation may never change to the point that they are able to do so.

Nevertheless, the cost of maintaining occasional contact with your "D-1"s and monitoring if and how their situation might change over time is minimal — and quite strategic considering the potential for them eventually doing business with you.

Maintaining Appropriate Contact

Going forward from your initial meeting or conversation, you're going to have minimal contact with "D-1" customers or sales leads — perhaps just once or twice a year and maybe just a brief call or email.

It won't take much of your time, but it can pay potential future dividends as you keep them involved with you until they are ready to make a purchasing decision — or you determine that it isn't likely to ever happen.

The key to maintaining effective contact with "D-1" customers or sales leads is to keep it infrequent and focus on maintaining the positive, professional relationship you established during your initial meeting or conversation.

They shouldn't feel any pressure to act because both you and they recognize that they won't be doing anything about what you offer for many months, if at all.

A "D-1" customer or sales lead won't suddenly turn into an "A-1" just because you and the customer want it to happen.

It has to run its course, but your contact with them will help you anticipate when their situation is changing to the point that they might be in a position to consider what you are offering.

The Purpose Of Your Contact

One of the chief reasons for maintaining contact, albeit infrequently, with your "D-1" customers and sales leads is to help insure that they remember you and your company so they will be inclined to want to do business with you if there ever comes a time when they are in a position to do so.

Remember also that they might be able to refer someone to you, and you want them to feel welcome to do that.

Your contact with your "D-1" customers and sales leads really has two purposes: the primary one is to keep your name in front of them (even if it is only once or twice a year), and secondarily, you need to be in a position to determine when their situation has changed to warrant a higher rating and more assertive action on your part.

Once you determine that a "D-1" customer or sales lead is able to consider what you offer, you can provide the appropriate amount of contact to help them make that decision.

7

Marking Outside The Lines

Other Types Of Contacts

So far, we've been concentrating on how you work with your customers, sales leads, and potential clients that come from conventional and traditional sources — newspaper or magazine ads, websites, online advertising, pay per click, organic searches, walk-in visits to your office or showroom, displays at trade or home shows, radio or TV, signage and billboards, coupons, and other types of marketing and promotion.

Add to that the sales leads you generate from mixers, receptions, business functions, association events, and referrals — plus direct contacts that you initiate.

After these people contact you or you meet them, you assign a score, grade, or mark to each one based on what you discover about their interest level in what you have to offer, the timing of when they would be willing to make a decision, and the likelihood or ability of them to make a decision.

When people like what you can offer well enough for them to consider working with you and your company — and quite possibly purchase from you — you add the suffix "1" to their "A," "B," "C," or "D" letter mark.

However, there are other types of leads and contacts that you'll want to note and keep track of — to provide a more complete picture of who you talk with and to guide you in your follow-up contact.

The types of contacts that we're going to look at briefly in this chapter are important to you and your business, but usually they will not be the ones who are making a buying decision with you. As such, they will not be receiving any of the traditional ratings that we've been discussing so far.

Nevertheless, they can be a powerful force for you in generating positive word-of-mouth marketing (WOMM) and referrals based on their perceptions and impressions of working with you and your company.

Recording The Contacts

Let anyone in these other categories that you will be creating learn about you and what you have to offer —

and make a record of who they are. Just count these contacts separately from your other customers and leads.

Don't count anyone as a customer — or assign a mark or grade to them — unless they actually are looking to do something for themselves.

Your discovery questions are important and will help you make the determination about the purpose of their contact and their level of interest. This is how you'll know whether to count them as some other category or as a regular customer or sales lead.

The Trades

The first group of people that you want to make a note of — outside of your traditional rating system — is the one that includes anyone associated with the building trades or construction industry.

This group we will designate "TRADES."

You as may fall into this category as a trade contractor, but there are many other trades, installers, and types of businesses that are part of this group that can be effective strategic partners for you.

This group does not include people like Realtors®, real estate brokers, architects, designers, or decorators.

They are in other groups.

Use "*trades*" to apply to people such as carpenters, electricians, roofers, plumbers, masons, siding installers, cement finishers, carpet and flooring installers, cabinet and countertop installers, dry wall installers and plasterers, tile setters and installers, painters, landscapers, and any other building or construction tradespeople except general contractors, home builders, renovators, or remodelers.

They may just want to learn more about what is going on in the market from your perspective, they may be interested in forming some type of strategic alliance or vendor relationship to provide services to you or your company, or they may have a customer for you.

Professionals

The next group of people that you want to make a note of is the one that includes anyone with some type of professional interest or affiliation with the real estate or construction industry or your specific business, industry, or organization.

This group we will designate "PROFESSIONALS."

You may be part of this group, but this is a large group of professionals. Reach out to the other professionals in the group, be receptive to strategic partnerships or alliances they want to create, and allow them to furnish leads and customers for you to work with — apart from them or by teaming up with them.

Use the term *"professionals"* for architects, attorneys, interior designers, decorators, kitchen and bath designers, appraisers, surveyors, landscape architects, model merchandisers, stagers, mortgage brokers, lenders, home builders, remodelers, consultants, new home sales professionals, non-profit organizations, ad agencies, health care professionals, inspectors, or other professionals.

Brokers

Use the term "BROKER" for any Realtor®, real estate broker, commercial real estate broker, commercial real estate agent, leasing agent, or other real estate professional who contacts you for general information about what you are doing in the marketplace or to discuss improvements you can make to a property they control or represent.

This category is just used to count the number of times any real estate agent (regardless of their actual title) contacts you when they are not trying to work with you on behalf of their clients or customers.

When a broker or real estate professional contacts or visits you with a client or customer intent on possibly using your services or purchasing something you are offering, they are the "source" and their customer is graded according to their particular level of interest and ability to make a decision — just as if they came to you from an ad, sign, your website, or other marketing.

In this case, count just the customer and not the broker in your traffic summary.

Third-Party

The next group of people that you want to make a note of is the one that we will designate "THIRD-PARTY." You might also want to label them "PROXY."

"*Third-party*" or "*proxy*" applies to someone who says that they are collecting information for someone else who is not present with them (cousin, boss, client, associate, friend, parent, grandparent, aunt or uncle, son or daughter, sibling, co-worker, trustee, financial advisor, committee, or neighbor).

They may really be doing as they say — looking for a product or service such as you offer and collecting information for their company or client, a friend, or relative who is not with them.

On the other hand, this may be just an excuse that they are using to keep from revealing too much information about their own needs.

Try to collect as much detail as you can about the absent person (their name and contact information — and their relationship to the person present on their behalf, as well as their general needs) while at the same time evaluating the possible interest of the "third-party" customer who is present.

Be aware that the "third-party" person may actually be disguising their own interest. If you suspect this to be the case, you should grade the "third-party" as a regular customer or sales lead with whatever information you can obtain.

Use a "C" or "C-1" rating as a good "default" starting point if you aren't sure what mark to give them.

Other

The last category of people that you want to make a note of is the one that we will call "OTHER" to apply to anyone else.

This can include someone making a delivery or someone who just stops in your office or showroom for directions or has general questions about the market or what you have available.

They could be someone whose establishment you visit on a regular basis, and they provide a referral for your to pursue based on what they know of your business.

Telephone Contacts

In addition to people who stop in your office or showroom, you will likely receive contact two other ways — by *telephone* and *email*.

When someone telephones for information, they may just want directions to your office, showroom, or event — having seen your phone number on a sign, billboard, or print ad. Maybe they visited your website.

They may be looking for a "mini-presentation" from you over the phone as they are trying to determine who to work with.

They may be trying to eliminate you from further consideration or keep you on their list just on the basis of what they learn during this phone call.

Obtaining Value From The Calls

Do your best to obtain the caller's name and their telephone number. Answer their questions, but do your own discovery at the same time.

As you learn about the customer or sales lead and their needs, write down their questions and responses on your information card or notepad.

There are many ways to obtain their telephone number.

One way is to tell your caller that you may think of something later that you wished you would have told them or a question comes to mind that you'd like to ask them to understand better what they want. You'll need a phone number to do this.

You can also use caller ID, but the person calling may be using a different number than you would use to reach them on a callback — or they might have the number blocked.

You can always just ask them for their phone number or confirm that the number they're calling you from is a good number to use to call them back. This gives you permission to call them as well.

If you aren't able to learn very much about the caller's needs on the initial call, a "C-1" is a good default rating because it assumes that they like you — and it will work until you learn enough about them to verify the mark or rating or adjust it as necessary.

Email Inquiries

Many people will email you directly from your website or from an ad or direct mail piece.

They may ask more about what you can do or what services you provide — even when this information is already on your website.

Or, they may have questions that will help them decide if they want to continue getting to know you and your company.

Part of this might be just to establish the initial contact and see how you respond to their request.

You won't necessarily be able to determine enough information to give someone a mark or letter grade that accurately reflects their level of interest or decision making ability — again, the "C-1" designation is a good starting point.

Starting an information card or notepad entry should be relatively easy.

Depending on what information your online contact form requires, you will have at a minimum their name and email address.

You may also be collecting their address, telephone number, and information about their needs.

Just as with all of the special categories discussed in this chapter, count telephone or email inquiries separately from your "walk-in" or direct contact customers or sales leads because they have not yet physically met with you.

8

Getting The Most From Your Customers & Sales Leads

Using Your Rating System

By this point, I know that you're going to have some type of a rating system to keep track of everyone you meet — customers, clients, and sales leads.

Maybe you haven't been using a formal rating system before reading this book, but you were just keeping track of the "good ones" in your head — or on a scratchpad, or on your phone, or in your computer.

Perhaps you haven't been paying that much attention to your other, less-good customers and sales leads.

Possibly, you've been using a rating system for just the "good" ones and dumped the majority of your sales leads and customers into the "C" or "D" or "NR" (not rated) categories — or left them unscored.

No matter where you have been in terms of keeping tabs on your customers and sales leads when you picked up this book and started reading it, you weren't getting the amount of impact out of your rating system that you should.

It's may be a little harsh to hear or read, but it's true. There is so much more you can be doing, and I think you've learned that from these pages.

In the system that you have been using — however formal or rudimentary it is — you didn't have the maximum ability to keep track of the people you were meeting or those contacting you to then schedule your time to work where you could be the most effective.

You haven't been efficient.

Now all that's changed.

Now you have the modified "**A-B-C + 1**" system.

It's time to make the switch from what you have been using — or to start using my system if you've just had an informal one prior to now.

Stop Chasing After People

Now, you have a very special rating system that lets you focus just on the people that like working with you. You can stop trying to "chase" after people that have no interest in considering or acquiring the product, service, or solution you are offering.

The issue with chasing after people has nothing to do with your persistence or diligence — or the quality of what you offer. It's them.

For whatever reason, they feel that their needs cannot be met by what you offer, or they don't relate to your approach for suggesting a solution to their needs.

When you chase after people, you usually end up frustrated because you get hardly any response from them — just unanswered phone calls, unreturned voice mail messages, and unanswered emails.

This is because they are intentionally eluding you.

They don't want to be contacted.

However, when you use the rating system that lets you use the "1" suffix after your mark of "A," "B," "C," or "D" — to denote people who like you and what you offer well enough to want to work with you — you can avoid investing time on uninterested people.

You can "chase" people all you want, but if you can't show people something they are interested in, or they don't like your approach, you're just not going to connect with them.

You will chase them further and further away and become exhausted in the process — with no sales to show for your efforts.

You run the risk of overlooking more interested customers and sales leads while you're chasing less qualified people, and you could be damaging your brand in the process.

Maximizing Your Effort

Rather than trying to chase after and track down people who are avoiding you because they have no real interest in what you are offering or in working with you, it makes sense to me for you to work with those people who have at least expressed an interest in wanting to work with you.

Doesn't this seem like a better use of your time?

The real reason you grade, rank, mark, or rate your customers and sales leads is so that you have a quick idea of generally where they are in the decision-making process, how you and your company factor into that process, and who you need to focus on the most.

There is nothing special or magical about rating people or in the mark or rank itself.

It's what the mark or rating represents and what it tells you about someone's relative degree of readiness to make a decision on what you are attempting to offer them that counts.

People change — be ready for it. Expect it. Anticipate it.

Their situations change. Their attitudes change.

Make sure their ratings or marks change as well — up or down, with a "1" added or removed.

Some people move closer to a decision, and some move further away.

Some people abandon their search entirely for a solution that your product or service can offer.

Likewise, someone who had seemed ready to make a quick decision when you met them, or during your initial conversation or presentation, may now be unable to do so for weeks or longer — if ever.

Some may get "caught-up" in the enthusiasm of your presentation and seem more interested in doing business with you or acquiring your product or service than they really are.

They may even try to convince themselves that they are more interested or closer to making a decision than actually is true.

Be Honest With Your Ratings

Don't be hasty in deciding which people you need to work with and which require a little additional attention from you. Let the ratings work for you.

Your assessment of someone's potential to do business with you and your company should never be based on emotion. Sometimes this is hard to remember.

You really want to achieve an accurate portrayal of the quality of your customers and sales leads and formulate an effective contact strategy for working with everyone.

This will range from almost daily contact for the "A-1," to less frequent contact for the "B-1," to infrequent contact for a "C-1," to virtually none for a "D-1" — and no meaningful contact for the "A," "B," "C," or "D".

It's easy to label or rate someone an "A" or "A-1" because it was pleasant talking with them, they were dressed well, or they seemed to share some of your same interests.

Never forget, however, that they have to meet the established criteria. It's that simple.

Don't be tempted to give someone an "A-1" rating or mark just because you like them or because you have empathy for their situation.

Don't give it because they are "nice" people or because you believe they will buy something from you as soon as their situation changes.

To be an "A-1" customer or sales lead, they must pass the test. They must fulfill all four criteria.

This does not mean that they are any better as a person than a "D-1" or any other customer or sales lead. It just means they are ready to make a buying decision now on something such as you offer — and that you can be the one to make the sale.

Remember the rating or mark has nothing to do with their personality or value as a person. It only signifies their relative ability to make a decision.

The Race Against The Clock

There is no prize for the company that can collect and amass the most "A-1" customers or sales leads.

This is not a contest. It's business.

This should never be your goal because you will only have one or two "A-1"s at any given time anyway.

"A-1"s in and of themselves don't pay anything. Closed transactions do.

The only difference between an "A-1" rating or mark and any other rating is that the "A-1" customer or sales lead is ready to make a decision — and capable of making one very soon. You stand a good chance of making the sale with them.

Remember that your "A-1" customers and sales leads are your best potential for a sale at any given moment, and that you only have a very short amount of time to capitalize on this opportunity — days or even hours.

For planning your post-visit follow-up program, figure that you have 3-4 weeks maximum to make a sale happen with an "A-1," but it's usually much less than that.

Actually, you may only have a day or two from when you initially meet or identify an "A-1" to make a sale with them — especially with solutions for traumatic conditions.

You're in competition with other salespeople and companies that also can meet this "A-1" customer's needs — and the clock is ticking.

Time is of the essence. You have to act quickly to make the sale happen.

You shouldn't appear to be desperate, just diligent.

The 30-Day Buying Cycle

The 30-day buying cycle is one of convenience. It's arbitrary.

However, if an "A-1" customer actually had a buying cycle that was 30 days long when they started seriously looking for a solution, they may be at or near the end of their cycle when they contact you for the first time.

They may have essentially made up their mind on what they want and where they are going to buy it before they ever contact you.

Literally, as they walk out the door and leave your office or showroom — or as you leave them if you arranged the appointment or presentation — their mind could be made up in favor of another salesperson or company even though they enjoyed meeting with you and liked what you had to say or what you showed them.

It could also be a case of them just not liking what you showed them or your approach — even though they are ready to make a decision. They might have been comparing what you had to say with another company or vendor that they had essentially decided on before meeting with or contacting you.

So, when you call them back a couple of days after their visit to you or your presentation with them, they may tell you that they already bought or decided on something else.

You may not really have 30-days to work with an "A-1" customer or sales lead — so plan accordingly and be prepared to act quickly.

If it's a conditions-based solution rather than a general renovation, the time for a decision may be quite short.

Planning For Your "A-1"s

To really understand where your "A-1" customers and sales leads are in their decision-making process and where you are in your follow-up contact with them, take the initiative and don't leave anything to chance.

Each morning as you start your sales day, review your notes on each "A-1" customer (the one or two that you have) so you are totally aware of what has transpired with each one and you are ready to make the sale.

It doesn't matter that you just looked at those cards and notes the day before, and the day before that. Look at them again.

Look at what still needs to happen for your "A-1"s to be able to say "yes" to your final closing question.

Then make certain that all planned contact with each

"A-1" customer is being accomplished and that no opportunities for contact are overlooked or lost.

You won't necessarily be contacting each "A-1" customer or sales lead every single day, but you need to be aware of what you have done and what still remains to be done with each one so you can plan and execute your next contact effectively.

Be ready for a phone call or email from them or a surprise, impromptu, drop-in visit to your office or showroom.

Just make sure that there are no surprises or missed opportunities and that you can take full advantage of each contact.

Managing The Rest Of Your Database

After you review your "A-1" customers and sales leads each day to make sure that you are current with everything, turn next to reviewing and monitoring your "B-1" and your "C-1" customers and sales leads.

Remember, many of your future "A-1" customers — and sales — will come from your customer database.

Depending on how many "B-1" customers and sales leads you have on file, plan on reviewing 25% or so each day until you've reviewed all of them within 3-4 days, then start over again.

Take a few more days to review all of your "C-1"s and then repeat.

If you have a relatively small amount of "B-1" and "C-1" customers and sales leads on file and you have the time to do so, you can review all of them or as many as you like each day.

As you have time, check your "D-1" customers as well.

Start with your "B-1" and "C-1" customers and sales leads who seem to have the highest probability of moving up to the next rank and strategize your follow-up contact to identify how to make that happen.

You have rated your "B" and "C" customers (without using the suffix "1") because they expressed little or no interest in working with you, so you won't schedule any regular contact with them.

However, as you are up-to-date with all of your other contacts, occasionally call a "B" or "C" customer to check on their status and determine how their search is going for a product or service such as you offer. Remember people are subject to change in both needs and life situations.

You might find out that they have been unsuccessful in

finding a solution for their needs and that they now would be willing to listen to what you offer. You then could then remark them as an "A-1," "B-1" or "C-1," as appropriate — to reflect their renewed interest in possibly working with you.

The Real Pay-Off

To maximize the results from using this rating system that I have given you, keep in mind that it is strictly objective, and as such will give you an unbiased profile of the relative decision-making strength and potential of your customers and sales leads — individually and collectively.

It is based on the "ready, willing, and able" test plus whether they "like" you and think you can help them.

It has no bearing on anyone's personality, how well you like them, or what you think of someone as a person.

You may "hit it off" with someone because you have similar personalities or enjoy common interests and are able to establish a great rapport with them.

Still, you should only rate them according to their ability to make a decision and not on how well you like them.

Conversely, if you do not relate to someone on a personal level, this is no reason to give them anything less than your highest rating — if they actually are ready to make a decision on what you offer and meet the test.

It's the criteria that matter and nothing else.

This marking system takes the personal element out of the rating — as long as you do a good job of discovery.

All it takes to rate someone's level of interest and ability to make a purchasing decision is for you to determine the answers to four very simple questions: are they *ready* to make a decision, are they *willing* to make a decision, are they *able* to make a decision, and do they *like* you well enough to work with you?

Your ability to get answers to those questions will directly impact how effective and efficient you are as a salesperson or businessperson.

You'll be able to concentrate and focus on the people with the highest ratings and de-emphasize those without the "1" rating.

The higher the rating, the closer you are to a sale.

It *is* that simple.

Steve Hoffacker

Steve Hoffacker, CAPS, MCSP, MIRM, is principal of Hoffacker Associates LLC, a sales training (new home sales, universal design, and aging-in-place) and coaching company based in West Palm Beach, Florida.

Steve is an award-winning, internationally-recognized and experienced new home salesperson and sales trainer, as well as a universal design/aging-in-place safety and accessibility sales trainer and instructor.

For more than 30 years, he has helped homebuilders, new home salespeople, contractors and remodelers, new home marketers, designers, architects, occupational therapists, and other professionals to be more visible, competitive, profitable, and effective — and to really enjoy themselves as they pursue their business and create wonderful customer experiences.

Steve wants you and your company to be successful and has created this guide (and many others) to help make that happen.

This book will be a great resource to help you take your business to another level and outpace the competition.

Use these strategies and concepts for your professional success.

www.ingramcontent.com/pod-product-compliance
Lightning Source LLC
Chambersburg PA
CBHW071438160426
43195CB00013B/1952